D1628369

MORE PREFAB DAYS

BELLE VALE REMEMBERS

First Published in Great Britain in 2008
by Enterprise Marketing and Publishing Services Ltd.
85-89 Duke Street, Liverpool, L1 5AP

ISBN 978-0-9554763-1-0

For all trade sales please contact
Enterprise Marketing & Publishing Services Ltd. on 0151 708 6822

Visit our website if you want to:

• Find out more about Belle Vale
• Meetings of Project
• Activities
• Post your memories of life in the Belle Vale prefabs
• Find old friends and neighbours

www.bellevaleprefabs.com

BELLE VALE REMEMBERS

Acknowledgements

Brenda Vale. Professor of Architecture at The University of Auckland.
Jon McDonagh.
All the members of Belle Vale Prefab Project who contributed to this book.
Christine Jones for providing financial services to the project.
Jill and Sid Jones, Belle Vale Post Office, for stocking and selling both books.
Thanks to Celia Kelly & Eddie Lansdowne, the working party for this book, for all their hard work, patience and imagination.

Typesetting by Joe McLaughlin
Edited by Paul Tarpey
www.defnetmedia.com

This book is the second collection of stories from
The Belle Vale Prefab Project, following on from the success of
Prefab Days (A Community Remembers), published in December 2006.
ISBN no. 978-0-9554763-0-3

More Prefab Days (Belle Vale Remembers) will be of interest as a
stand alone book, but also to complement the first book.

If you are interested in the first book it can be purchased through
Amazon.co.uk, the Belle Vale Post Office,
Enterprise Marketing & Publishing Services Ltd.
On 0151 708 6822. Email empsltd@btconnect.com
Or by contacting bvpp@blueyonder.co.uk.

THE FAB PREFABS

I remember it well - we moved in on a Monday
Our next door neighbour was Councillor Cundy.
The first thing to do was look around and explore
To see the facilities we all have in store.

A few yards away we had four lovely shops.
The first was the butcher with his beef and pork chops.
The greengrocer next with his fruit and his greens
With spuds and tomatoes and runner beans.
Next to him was George Adams' store:
Groceries, bread and biscuits galore.

Then there was Harry Cable he sold cigarettes and sweets
Balloons and comics and other kids' treats.
He was a nice chap and became every one's mate
And if you were skint gave cigs on the slate.
It was a great help in those early stages
You could pay your bill when you got your wages.

The window cleaner whistled as he went on his rounds.
We soon got used to the familiar sounds
But to look at his tools what could be sadder
He only had three rungs on his ladder!
So all in all it was easy to tell
He wouldn't hurt himself even if he fell.
The kids all loved him as he went around the streets
For he always had a pocket full of sweets.

The Community Centre was not far away
And was very well organised from day to day.
Saturday night was the old films but the best
We saw Four Feathers and even Beau Geste.
We watched Tarzan in his many escapes
Johnny Weissmuller, Jane and their apes.
We watched these films and never went to town.
For a family of four it was just half a crown.
When we went in we had biscuits and tea
For no charge at all it was the very same fee.

We also had kiddies' colourful prancers
Entertainment provided by our own Morris dancers
So come on folks with the Prefab Tradition
Make sure you see our next edition!

By Harold Citrine, 3 Crossbrooke Road

FOREWORD
By Professor Brenda Vale

Brenda is currently Professor of Architecture at The University of Auckland in New Zealand. She is an architect, writer and researcher, whose interest in the Belle Vale project goes way beyond an uncanny co-incidence in terms of her name. Her book "Prefabs: The History of the UK Temporary Housing Programme", alongside several books about sustainable housing shows her interest in how housing and planning best serve people and their environment. She is currently engaged in highly successful research into sustainable housing that can be built with no fuel costs, and was happy to write the introduction to a book about a community that she sees as pioneering in many ways.

I have been looking at prefabs for so long, it is hard to know how it all started. As a child I recall being taken to visit a family in east London who lived in a prefab (we lived in Ilford) but most of this memory is about there being lots of children to play with, presumably not all from the same house. I have another childhood memory of the hearth unit of a prefab in the Science Museum at Kensington where the copper tank had been polished and thinking how lovely it looked.

I am also aware that talking to people about prefabs nearly always brought forth some positive memory of living in one, or knowing someone who did. What I wanted to find out was why people liked them and also why they had survived for so many years beyond their design life. I don't think I became an architect because of the prefabs but perhaps because my Dad was a town planner and I remember being shown round a very windy Harlow new town that he wanted to see, though that might have been more likely to put me off.

I also remember Mum telling us stories about making Spitfire engines in the war, which we thought was very glamorous and it must have been a come down for her staying at home to look after me and my younger sister. Dad spent his war in Burma but he never talked about that at all. I don't think he had any good memories though I did find some photos of him and his mates smiling, wearing shorts and looking very thin and brown, many years afterwards. Maybe my wish to be involved with the prefabs was a way of getting closer to Mum and Dad and the awful experiences they had then and the lovely people they remained despite them.

"I shan't feel really happy about the temporaries unless one of the fixtures in each of them is a fifteen-year-time-bomb guaranteed not to be a dud."
(BBC, 1944, Homes for All, Littlebury, Worcester, p.17)

The 1944 Temporary Housing Programme gave birth to the prefabs. During World War II lack of house building and house repair created a housing shortage, as materials and man power were directed to the war effort. Bombing had also destroyed houses in targeted towns and cities, such as Liverpool, creating increased local demand. The hope was that prefabrication would somehow solve these problems by moving production from the vagaries of the site to the factory, where the process would be speeded up under cover, with less wastage of materials because of more controlled conditions. To meet immediate needs, the government of the time embarked on a programme of prefabricated temporary houses, hence 'prefabs', with a 10-15 year life.

The public first heard of prefabs during a March 1944 Sunday radio broadcast by Prime Minister Winston Churchill. He discussed what was to happen to housing supply after the war.

Two approaches were proposed. The first was repair of damaged houses, work that was to be started almost immediately, and the second was provision of, "...prefabricated or emergency houses...I hope we may make up to half a million of these." He went on to say that these half a million houses would make use of the products of a steel industry that had been significantly expanded for the war effort. Thus what was to become the UK Temporary Housing Programme, under which 156,623 prefabricated two bedroom bungalows were produced in 1945-1949, was started not just to provide much needed homes but also to give employment in factories to soldiers returning from the war. The Beveridge Report on the welfare state had promised that there would be full employment after the war, along with access to health care, education, housing, and pensions for all.

The prototype prefab designed by the Ministry of Works, which was called the Portal Bungalow after the Minister Lord Portal and exhibited at the Tate Gallery, was all steel. The architect was CJ Mole who worked for the Ministry. In fact there was no surplus of steel after the war, partly because of the extended war with Japan, and other materials had to be found to meet Churchill's vision. Various groups put forward proposals, including firms like Uni-Seco who had built huts for the war, and eventually 13 types of prefab were approved including 8,462 imported from the USA under the lend-lease scheme and 50 brick 'prefabs' for the Isle of Lewis, where the climate was severe.

The aluminium bungalows used on the Belle Vale Estate were built on a production line by the aircraft industry and were the most automated in terms of their construction. The aircraft industry had expanded massively in the war and was looking for other products to make in peace time. Five factories were involved in their production: the Bristol Aeroplane Co., Weston-super-Mare; Vickers-Armstrong, at both Blackpool and Chester; Blackburn Aircraft, Dumbarton; and A.W. Hawksley,

Gloucester. This scattering of production was a legacy of the war where production was arranged in this way so that if one factory was bombed, others would keep going. More aluminium bungalows were produced (54,500) than any other type even though they were also the most expensive. A prototype, made at Weston-super-Mare, was exhibited behind Selfridge's at the 'Aluminium War to Peace Exhibition' in 1945. The aluminium prefabs were made in four sections complete with all internal fittings, services and final decoration. Dimensions were determined by the maximum width that could be delivered by road, making sections 7ft 6in wide and 22ft 6½in long. These were delivered to the site and each part lifted into place with a 5 ton crane and it was claimed that crews could complete the site assembly in 30-40 hours. The structural frame was extruded aluminium, panels were of aluminium insulated with aerated concrete and the floor was timber joists bolted to the aluminium frame and finished with tongue and grooved boards.

The prefabs only had two bedrooms because they were always thought of as temporary, and would be replaced as soon as the building industry returned to full strength and could build permanent homes. For this reason they were often placed on odd vacant bits of land or on sites earmarked for permanent housing estates to be built later. However, the fact that so many prefabs lasted well beyond their 10-15 year design life can be attributed not only to their construction but because they provided a housing type people wanted. Towards the end of the war when it was obvious that the Allies would eventually be victorious, there were a number of surveys asking people what housing they wanted to live in post war. The most sought after house was the detached house in its own garden. Bungalows were also popular. Few people thought a flat would be their ideal house. The small prefab sitting in its own piece of garden was the house the people wanted, never mind that it was made of strange materials like aluminium or was built in a factory, so it is no surprise that some have lasted 60 years or that people have fond memories of them.

The prefabs should also be regarded as pioneers in the modern quest for a more sustainable environment. They had gardens where food could be grown, they could be insulated (many were by local authorities), they had space and a shed in which to mend things, they were simple to maintain, they even had a generous roof area that could now be used for solar energy equipment. They provided a resilient environment where people could do things for themselves. The prefabs were the kind of house people wanted, but what they were provided with as permanent homes were often flats. Flats are ideal for a consumer society where the aim is to sell people as much as possible, because what people can do for themselves in a flat is often very limited. The fact that what people remember about the prefabs is the sense of living in a community, the sharing that the prefabs provided, should be recalled by those who are designing the sustainable houses and communities of the future.

Brenda Vale
September 2008

PREFAB CHILDHOOD

I am a 1950 baby from a prefab in Belle Vale
Born at 41 Bridgefield Road (on the corner of Cloverdale).

There were four of us in the family — my father and my mother
And eight and a half years older than me was Philip,
my big brother.

I went to Joseph Williams from '55 to '62.
I loved it and even went there for Sunday School lessons too.

Happy summers on my bike, riding round Belle Vale,
Winters were very cold and we got firewood from Miss Quayle.

There were the shops in Bridgefield Road, the church and,
of course, the park.
Friends and I had a den there and would play till it got dark.

Winters we would stay indoors and watch a small TV.
I loved all the cowboys — from the Lone Ranger to Laramie.

Belle Vale was such a happy place — just like a holiday camp.
We didn't care that each winter the prefabs were so damp!

The valley would fill with fog — thick and very grey
But, if you could get to the Fiveways, it was likely a sunny day!

We were moved in 1966 from Belle Vale to Cantril Farm Estate.
It wasn't what we wanted and was a place we came to hate.

A childhood in the prefabs was the best I could have had.
They were such happy days with our Phil and Mum and Dad.
The three of them had moved there in the winter of `47
The worst winter in many years but the prefab seemed like heaven.

I've nothing but happy memories of those special Belle Vale years
So let's all celebrate with this second book and to all of you, three cheers!

By Jean Young, 41 Bridgefield Road

PART ONE

The first edition of this book saw a remarkable response from those linked to Belle Vale and beyond. It saw members of the group appearing on radio and in local newspapers, and they were also sought to speak at many meetings of community and history groups. We have also quite recently become aware of its importance as a reference for students of both architecture and social history.

In producing a second book, we knew how much we wanted to keep the human story that existed in the first book, but also to talk about the politics surrounding the Belle Vale Prefab Estate. The more you read about this unusual community and try to unravel why the memories here are so powerful, the more fascinating stories you find.

The roots of the Belle Vale Estate started with Churchill's fear of social unrest after the Second World War. He knew that the conditions that ex-servicemen were resigned to at the end of the First World War were a major reason for the discontent that followed at that time and 'The Temporary Housing Programme' was designed to deal with this potential threat.

In 1943 the Ministry of Works was set up to organise the requisitioning of property for wartime use, but they retained responsibility for Government building projects after the war. It was this ministry that developed a 6.5 acre site in Northolt with thirteen blocks of different styles of temporary housing built under the direction of chief architect C.J. Mole. He was advised by an independent panel, including Liverpool's innovative Chief Architect and Director of Housing; Lancelot Keay. Keay was later to play a significant part in estates such as Kirkby and Speke. The Ministry of Health set up a similar group of houses in Sighthill, Edinburgh and the Building Research Station in Albert's Close, Hertfordshire.

This research appeared to lead to a dispute between the Ministry of Health and the Ministry of Works. The Ministry of Health felt that greater research and a broader approach was needed. They wanted more efficient housing that could deal with the needs of expanding post-war families. It may have been felt that houses with a lifespan of ten years would take resources away from this longer term housing problem.

Whatever the exact nature of this dispute it was soon decided that a quick programme of easily constructed homes, dealing with the homelessness of ex-servicemen and the needs of a damaged industry, was unavoidable.

The local authority could purchase these homes at ten shillings each from the government and charge the same rent as they did to their more permanent tenants elsewhere. It seems the potential long term problems were less important when the new estate suited both the local authority's pockets and central government's agenda.

The Liverpool Corporation had identified an area of countryside that was large enough for a massive housing project and was still just inside Liverpool's boundaries. Then the homes started to arrive at an amazing rate; the war had left them well trained in dealing with crisis situations. Priority was given to those injured in the war, but family needs were also taken into account, and the Belle Vale estate started to take shape.

The memories that follow echo many in the first book, but also act as a companion, and much of the information provided attempts to fill gaps the group felt existed after the first publication.

FIRST IMPRESSIONS

"you will love it, and you won't have to go to the public baths any more"

In 1946-7, as a newly married couple, my wife and I lived with her parents, as many couples did just after the war. The back of the house in Corbridge Road overlooked the Childwall Fiveways. No pub in those days, just a big emergency water supply tank, and no roundabout, just an open roadway with a lamp standard in the centre. We watched with envy as trailer after trailer went past the Fiveways down Childwall Valley Road carrying parts of prefabs to the new housing estate in Belle Vale. We were envious because our War Service did not qualify for a high priority on the housing list.

Donald Headey

Prefab Construction

The prefabs were built mostly for servicemen returning from the war. We thought we were moving into five star luxury; hot running water, a bath, fridge and electric cooker. We had been used to boiling the kettle and pans on the fire, and using a tin bath in front of the fire. The only downside was that they were freezing cold in the winter. Coal was rationed as well. We didn't have electric blankets then. We had a small paraffin heater which we kept in the hall.

Barbara Flynn nee Berriclough
21 Braehurst Road

We moved into 29 Bridgefield Road in 1947. There were no fences around the gardens and we had to walk a plank across a ditch as the pavements hadn't been done. While Joseph Williams School was being built, we used to play hide and seek in the large pipes that were there.

Taylor Family
29 Bridgefield Road

L-R Irene Edwards, L Taylor & June Edwards 1954. 29 Bridgefield Rd

Chuck, John & Rob Smith, 71 Braehurst Rd

In March 1947 I moved from Garston to a prefab at 71 Braehurst Road. I was six years old and the place was magic for me. We had been living in my grandad's old gas lit terraced house in Garston with a variety of relatives. Suddenly we had everything newly built and we were surrounded by plenty of space to roam.
Chuck Smith
71 Braehurst Rd.

I was eight years old when we moved into our prefab. We had been living in a two room flat and it was like coming into a brand new world. I remember asking my mother, 'What's a prefab?' 'You will see,' she said. 'You will love it, and you won't have to go to the public baths any more.'
Brian Nolan
23 Sunnyfield Road

I do remember when we lived in St. Helens in a fireman's flat belonging to Pilkington's. Dave had left Lancashire County Fire Service because I was pregnant and we couldn't afford the mortgage on the terraced house we had in Mossley Hill. The mortgage was £13 a month and we never had the money to pay it. The pay at Pilkington's was good but unfortunately Dave hated the job and he realised he had made a mistake. He said he felt like a Keystone Cop. Finally Dave wrote to Lancashire County and asked them to take him back. They slapped his wrists then fished out his old uniform from stores, reduced his pay, told him not to do it again and took him back.

When Dave gave his notice in, Pilkington's Solicitors wrote to us and gave us seven days' notice to quit the flat. The law was a lot different then and we just had to get out. I was eight months pregnant at the time and it was two weeks before Christmas. Dave was to be stationed at Widnes Fire Station, so we spent days walking around Widnes trying to get accommodation. We had no luck and I needed to book in somewhere to have the baby, so days before Christmas we moved back in with my mother in the Belle Vale prefabs in Charlwood Road. They were already in the process of being demolished and my mum knew that she was waiting for a promised one bedroomed flat on the Netherley estate. We knew the arrangement was temporary but we all hoped that my mum would not have an offer of a flat until after the baby was born and we could find somewhere to live.

About a week later, when Mum and Dave were at work, a gentleman called. He told me he was the rent man from the Corporation Housing department and informed me that they had received a complaint that we had moved back in with my mum and it was thought that we intended to try and get a corporation house for us all to share. He told me that I could stay until my baby was born but that my husband had to go that very day. He said Dave could visit during the day but under no circumstances could he stay the night. He also told me that if we didn't do as we were told then my mum would be refused her flat too. Mum and I had lived together in the prefab since my father had died almost ten years earlier, and I would never have done anything to threaten her home. I remember how upset we all were.

Dave went to his mum's in Garston at first, but he started to stay at the Fire Station during the period when he did nights. After Anna was born we tried for rented property without success, and then, when Anna was about eight weeks old, Dave was offered the key to rented fire service property in Leigh. Apparently they were all fed up with him sleeping at the fire station.

Freda Heathcote nee Mahoney
12 Charlwood Road

Freda Mahoney with Timmy the Dog. 12 Charlwood Road

My family came from Stone, Staffordshire. It was just after the war and we lived with my grandmother. My father worked at the English Electric in Stafford and they had jobs on East Lancashire Road and workers could transfer. We were offered a house with the job, hence our move to Liverpool and our own house. I was three when we came here and my brother was born in Gateacre. We moved to Maghull when I was fourteen. We had many happy years in our prefab (fitted kitchen, lovely bathroom, loads of storage space set in our own garden). In Maghull there are a few prefabs which have been bricked up and modernised, and look wonderful. Pity this couldn't have happened years ago in Gateacre.
Wendy Hocter nee Bloom
63 Belle Vale Road

A detached bungalow with its own grounds is how I remember the prefabs. Number 2 Endbrook Road was everything a six year old could wish for. A large garden with a park over the back fence where you could play football all day and night. Mum marvelled at the kitchen, a built in fridge, wash boiler and cooker with built in cupboards and a larder, add to that wonderful neighbours who had all gone through a tough time during the war.
Harry Robertson
2 Endbrook Road

Sue Corness Christening 1947. 14 Charlwood Rd

It was heaven to have a bathroom and hot water heated by the fire, and not have to go down the yard to the toilet. The first thing we did was to have a bath (what luxury) but couldn't agree who was to go first, so we both jumped in together!
Edna Corness
14 Charlwood Road

In the summer of 1948 the country started the National Health Service. At the same time a young pharmacist, David Francomb, opened the only Chemist shop in the area at 19, Hedgefield Road.

The immediate post-war rules and regulations resulted in all construction work needing a permit. The result of that was that when he opened the shop, it had a counter, but all the traditional mahogany display cupboards and fittings were stacked up against one wall awaiting a permit for the wood to mount them on.

The dispensary was even worse, there was only a sink with cold water, so David started dispensing medicines and making ointments on planks propped up on packing chests. It was three months before the pharmacy reached the high professional standards he always maintained and continued for nearly twenty years until the shops were closed to make way for the shopping centre.

There were very few telephones in the prefabs and the pharmacy phone was in frequent use for emergency calls, like calling an ambulance, contacting the midwife and enquiries to the hospitals to ask about the seriously ill. He was often called on to recommend treatment of sick animals, sometimes even being asked to sex litters of pups and kittens.

In 1950, before I met David, I was employed as a social worker for Liverpool Personal Services who were agents for the Royal Navy Benevolent Trust and the Royal Alfred Mercantile Marine Trust. A high proportion of the original prefab tenants were ex-servicemen who were disabled and needed single story accommodation. Many were sailors who had their feet or fingers amputated due to frostbite as a result of sailing or being torpedoed on convoy duty. Amputations resulted in the loss of balance and inability to get employment, as many employers thought they were either drunk or suffered from fits. As a result, some needed financial assistance from the benevolent funds.

My job gave me the privilege and delight at being invited into the houses to help with filling forms and checking entitlement. The prefabs were new, carefully looked after and sometimes with little furniture. Some wives were Scandinavian and German with original ways of planning the rooms, and were also good housewives. Everyone seemed so delighted with their prefab; wherever they had come from, there was a strong community spirit. The gardens were beautiful, many growing vegetables as well as flowers and most of the winners of the City's awards went to the Belle Vale prefabs. It was a delight to walk around the area with beautiful gardens, no litter, no cars or vandalism.

We enjoyed our years in Hedgefield Road but had to close the pharmacy when the shops were demolished. After a period as a manager, David again opened a shop from scratch in Tarbock Road. He died in December 1986 after a long illness.
Paula Francomb nee McGoff

SETTLING IN

"we stopped digging when the prefab foundations were in danger"

Ruth Otterson marries Gordon Roberts, 1960. 4 Whinhurst Rd

My father, Robert Otterson, was a regular soldier. Our family had moved to Liverpool from Catterick in December 1947, living first in "digs" with a Mrs Leather, just a few doors down from St Peter's Church in Woolton. When the army quarters were ready, we moved to Crossacres Camp, situated between Speke Road and School Lane. In July 1949, Dad was killed in a motorcycle accident on his way home from army camp in Wales, leaving Mum with three children. I was ten, my sister Ann was eight and my brother, Michael, was a nine month old baby. Our family moved to number 4, Whinhurst Road on the "prefab estate" shortly afterwards.

Ruth Roberts nee Otterson
4 Whinhurst Road

We moved to our prefab in April 1957, that is me, my eldest daughter Valerie and my lovely baby Janet who was only six weeks old. Val had just turned twenty months. My husband Bob was in Fazakerley Hospital suffering from TB, but he was due to be discharged around June. It was tough for me at the time and I was only twenty years old, but I struggled on visiting my beloved Bob in hospital, trying to put my home together and coping with two little ones. It was no easy task.

I was on the verge of a breakdown and my mother suggested I move back , "just till Bob gets home", but I was not having any of that. Oh no. I had fallen in love with my prefab. It was my first real house and it had almost everything in it; built in wardrobes, a modern bathroom (like I had never seen before), a fitted kitchen with fridge, a boiler and wringer (both concealed) and loads of cupboards. Oh I wasn't leaving this place! Anyway, my brother and his wife and family only lived in Cloverdale Road, so I could spend an hour or two at theirs from time to time.

Bob did come home in June and what a homecoming it was. He walked in the door and said, "Our own little house, two lovely daughters and a lovely, lovely wife. What more could a man wish for?"

Bob was getting better all the time. He kept up with the medication and the time was getting near for him to return to work with the Fire Service. We didn't have much money but it didn't seem to matter so much: we were happy. In fact I don't recall any unhappy memories while living in that house. Twenty months after Bob came home from hospital I gave birth to our third daughter, Carol.

The friendliness amongst the neighbours was great and we had a lot of laughs too. I can remember once asking Carol to get down the avenue to Elsie our neighbour and ask if she had some disinfectant to lend me. Now Carol had a slight stutter so it made things a little difficult. The next thing was Elsie shouting; 'Hey, Doris! What is all this about 'dick infectant?' Well, you can imagine; the windows all shot open and the laughter was never ending.

Doris Tinman
19 Sunnyfield Road

Doris Tinman, Janet & Carol, 1960. 19 Sunnyfield Rd

Before the prefab we lived in a top floor flat in Dingle. My uncle was moving from his prefab and offered the key to my dad for the costly sum of £100. My dad, having two young boys and wanting to live in the country as he called it, paid the money and moved in. This was probably not legal but the corporation accepted the story of the exchange.

My dad, having an Irish farming childhood, loved it, but my mum, from under the bridge in Garston, found the separation from her roots difficult to adjust to.
My brother Patrick and I loved it; apparently we dug the garden up and annoyed neighbours by picking their flowers. We eventually stopped digging when the prefab foundations were in danger.
Mike Axworthy
17 Whinhurst Road

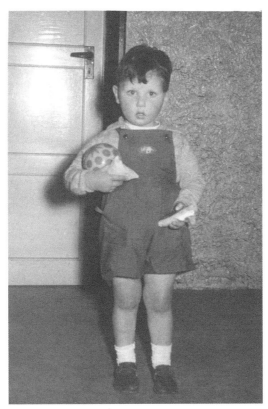

Philip Luxon, 55 Charlwood Rd with Coronation Party Gift in Labour Club

My husband Gerry, our young son Philip aged 17 months and I moved into a prefab in November 1952 for which we were very thankful as our other possible choice was a flat in Speke! The rent was 17s.5d per week, how much in decimal? 87p I think. We were very glad of it as it was our first real home and Gerry was recovering from a serious illness. The only drawback was winter and the prefab was cold, so everything possible covered the bed to keep us warm.

We had a living room with a coal fire, a fully fitted kitchen which included a fridge, very few people could boast of that, a boiler, a cooker, and large enough to have a table and chairs, a bathroom and two reasonably sized bedrooms and a hall. The prefab was detached with a garden all around. There were 1159 prefabs, and we had farms around us. There were two schools, Joseph Williams and Besford Road. A Catholic school was in the process of being built.

We settled down in 55 Charlwood Road and gradually got to know the neighbours. Under our circumstances we met many kindnesses from the community, which was what it was, we had a lot of support and help with decorating and gardening and in other ways which we appreciated very much. In 1953, the year of the Coronation,

Gerry Luxon with son Philip

we hadn't lived there twelve months, when a weekly collection was made to have a party for the children in the Labour Club. Nobody had knocked at our door to collect but on the day there was a knock asking Philip to the party. Although I protested we hadn't contributed, they weren't concerned. We have a picture of him with his gift of a ball under his arm and sandwiches in his hands and looking very shy!

The Labour Club was already built by the time we went to live there, it was just up the path from us. I understand it was built by the men living on the estate as a place for community functions. Some men who had been in the war and were working gave their time evenings and weekends.

Gerry was given an invalid (Noddy) car which he had to drive down our avenue. The avenue was also used by the neighbours to get to the bus stop for the Number 79 bus.

After some time we heard the prefab next but one to ours was becoming vacant. It was at the other end of the avenue with easy access to a garage from the road. I saw the local councillor who lived on the estate, to ask him to recommend us for it as it would make life easier and safer. We were eventually told it was ours. As we waited to be told officially we were informed, on good authority from a neighbour who knew everything, that a family from elsewhere had been given it. Nobody could believe it, all the neighbours supported us. The new people came along on the Friday night; they brought what they could in their car.They brought groceries and laid carpet ready for their furniture to come the next day, but when the van came there wasn't a thing left in the prefab. Everything had mysteriously disappeared in the night. They decided not to take the prefab after all and we were then given it. I don't know to this day what happened and as far as I know nobody else knows. You can draw your own conclusions!
Joan Luxon
55 Charlwood Road

Early in 1948 my mum and dad were allocated one of these prefabs and moved in with their two daughters. I was 17 months old and my little sister had just been born. These homes were intended only as a temporary solution to the housing problems after the war but in fact they were not demolished until the sixties.

It was an idyllic childhood in which I was blissfully unaware of the horrors of the Second World War. It was not until my teenage years that I realised Dad had been a prisoner of war for most of that time. Some of the best years of his life had been stolen from him by the war and he returned home a somewhat broken man. For him and for my mother the years spent in the prefab were an opportunity to forget, to immerse themselves in family life and provide a future for their children. They both worked hard in a time which began with ration books and when, as my Mum said, they were always thinking of ways to 'raise a few bob'.

For the 'baby boomers', who grew up together on an estate of over one thousand houses, life was an adventure. We enjoyed more freedom than today's children, exploring our rural surroundings and forging many enduring friendships.

Sue Wilding nee Benson
42 Whinhurst Road

Susan & Moya Benson August 1958. 42 Whinhurst Rd

Coronation Pageant June 1953. Wales Belle Vale School

When I began to teach at Belle Vale, in September 1952, the school had been open for just one term. Numbers were growing as children who lived near the school transferred from Joseph Williams School and Gateacre C of E School.

My class consisted of eight top year juniors (11 plus), twelve 10 plus and twenty 9 plus, three year groups in one classroom! Quite a challenge - but the children were well-behaved (on the whole) and keen to learn. So we coped for a year until the intake allowed a full class in each age group.

The young lady who taught the 8+ class was a very competent pianist who played for morning assembly and singing lessons. When her probationary period was over she moved on to another school and the Head Teacher (Mr Robert Quayle) had to call an emergency meeting to find which member of the staff would or could take the piano stool. To my dismay I was the only one who had studied music - and that was for twelve months at Sefton Park (Emergency) Teacher Training College. I had to keep telling myself, "If I'm the only one - I must be the best! In the country of the blind, the one-eyed man is king."

We sang "The Lord's My Shepherd" and "What Shall We Do With A Drunken Sailor?" until I extended my repertoire. I used to pick out the melody with the right hand and fit an appropriate chord with the left hand.

1953 was Coronation Year and every Liverpool school was invited to train a choir to sing some chosen songs. The choirs would then join together to sing at a concert of massed choirs at the Liverpool Stadium, conducted by Mr. Jenkins, the education authority's musical advisor. It was a great occasion and a wonderful experience for the children to travel into the city and walk through some of the city streets. Some found it hard to believe that people actually lived in some of the dingy tenement blocks and had to be shown that there were curtains on some of the windows and smoke was coming from the chimneys.

Donald Headey

Marjorie Wood, 1961 New pumping station in background. 93 Sunnyfield Rd

I was absolutely delighted with my prefab; it was like a holiday home. It had all modern conveniences; fitted kitchen with wash boiler, fridge, cooker and hot and cold water. What a boon. The kitchen was large enough to have parties for the girls with up to twelve children seated around the table. The bathroom was a great asset; hot water to have baths at any time, in fact it was the warmest room in the prefab because it contained the airing cupboard with hot water cylinder. It had two bedrooms, each with fitted wardrobes and cupboards which were made of steel as were the window frames. The hall was quite large and big enough to take a full sized pram. I thought the garden was marvellous as it gave the children somewhere to play on green grass. No need for the park.

Most of my neighbours were young families like us, so we made lots of friends and the children always had someone to play with. We had lots of visits from friends and relations who enjoyed being able to bring their children to play in the garden. The children could always have a bath before going home.

The only downside was that they were extremely cold in the winter; it was not unusual to have ice on the inside of the windows. The original intention was that the fire would provide central heating through warm air ducts into the bedrooms but this didn't work hence the reason they were so cold. Most people like me tried to keep warm with paraffin heaters. Despite this I was still very happy in my prefab and I never wanted to leave. In 1966 as they were demolished I actually cried.
Marjorie Thomas
93 Sunnyfield Road

Granny Heys. 109 Charlwood Rd

In 1947 we moved from a flat in Lodge Lane to a lovely prefab. How excited I was with my own fridge, cooker, boiler and all fitted units. It was Heaven! A wonderful place to raise my daughters Carol and Julia. My husband Rob was a disabled ex-serviceman who was never happier than when relaxing in the garden during those wonderful summers.

The day we moved in Gran Heys from 109 Charlwood Road brought over tea and scones while my husband Rob was waiting for the furniture to come. She was a lovely old lady, we all loved her. She was typical of all the neighbours I had while living there.
Nellie Crookham
103 Charlwood Road

PLANNING A COMMUNITY
By Jon McDonagh

Jon is currently researching Government schemes of community building on large scale council estates 1930-80 at Oxford University.

Liverpool Corporation always liked to think of itself as a pioneer in public housing. The city was, after all, home of the world's first council flats: St Martin's Cottages, Vauxhall, built in 1869. By the 1930s, it was attracting visitors from around the world eager to learn from its progressive Housing Department. The City Architect, Lancelot Keay, saw himself as a builder of communities not just houses and he sought to learn lessons from failed estates such as Norris Green. At Speke, as in its sister project in Kirkby, it was sought to mix middle and working class residents in council-owned homes, and provide a magnificent town centre to instil civic pride.

It was, of course, the Second World War that halted progress in Speke and made it necessary for Belle Vale to be built. Liverpool's housing shortage, which had been severe in 1939, was critical by 1945. The Liverpool Post reported on 28th February 1945: 'If the fringe of the city's housing problem is to be cleared, 15,000 dwellings must be provided in the next two years.' Keay could no longer afford to experiment with his idealistic schemes and Belle Vale was laid out as economically as its site allowed. The estate provided as many houses as possible – and its street pattern lacked the grand public spaces which had been planned for Speke.

Belle Vale was a rather unloved project within the Housing Department. Indeed Lancelot Keay resented any prefabs being built in Liverpool after his entry in a Government competition for prefab designs lost out to the type seen in Belle Vale. In early 1945 he had erected his own prototype 'narrow-fronted bungalow' in Church Street car park to display what he intended to build. However, in an era of strict rationing it was the Ministry of Health that would have the final say and Nye Bevan, as the responsible minister, claimed Keay's model was 'simply not practical'.

On top of this it became apparent that Belle Vale would demand far higher maintenance costs than most other areas of council property. At a stormy town hall meeting in July 1948, one councillor alleged that; 'At Belle Vale, 65 men, whose job it is to look after 1,159 temporary bungalows and 563 permanent buildings, are necessitating a yearly wage bill of £22,000.' This was out of a city-wide maintenance budget of £50,000. It seemed particularly wasteful to spend so much money on an estate which was scheduled to be replaced as soon as possible.

It is precisely because Belle Vale was an accidental and unwanted child of Liverpool's housing policy that it demands so much attention. In fact its residents fared much better than other inhabitants of prefabs across the city. Those who lived in the prefabs bordering Speke, for example, were treated with hostility by their neighbours. These war-time huts were soon regarded as eyesores, and the families inside as unwanted intruders on the green belt. Children from the prefabs were blamed for causing vandalism and their parents accused of being lazy gardeners.

It was surely the size of the Belle Vale prefab community which gave it a sense of solidarity. Shared experience was the crucial bond between neighbours. Indeed, given the fact that most council-inspired schemes of 'community building' have failed, we might think that shared experience is the only thing which can bring a newly-established community together.

Fifty years ago, a Liverpool University study of an estate matching Belle Vale's description concluded: 'The social characteristics of fellow-residents on a housing estate (particularly neighbours) are at least as important as the design of the individual house and the layout of a town as a whole so far as personal relations and friendships are concerned.'* I think the experiences recounted in this book show that they are far more important.

The word 'community' means different things to different people. However, the community recalled in this book is probably the sort that matters most in day-to-day life, and is certainly what people miss most when it has gone. History should make us very suspicious when any public authority claims it can build 'community'. Indeed this might be a task we would prefer government not to attempt at all. The expert is next door.

*Black and Simey, (Eds.), Neighbourhood and Community (Liverpool University Press, 1954), p.8.

Site	Uni-Seco	Phoenix	Alum.	Liverpool	Arcon	U.S.A
Ashfield	8					
Belle Vale			1159			
Carisbrooke Road	16					
Cherry Lane	29					
Creswick Street	21					
Dovecot	49					
East Prescot Road			16			
Finch House	262					
Fitzclarence Street	22					
Foley Street	31					
Fountains Road	50					
Gillmoss			213		138	58
Gt. Homer Street	32					
Haggerston Road			18			
Larkhill				2		
Lewisham Road	20					
Lister Drive			97			
Long Lane, Garston	28					
Longmoor Lane			43			
Longview Farm			76			
Lower Breck Road			9			
Minshull Street	34					
Muirhead Avenue	8					
Peter Road	39					
Prescot Street	54					
Rathbone Street	12					
Richard Kelly Drive	108					
Rollo Street	7					
Rosalind Street	74					
Sheil Park			73			
Sparrow Hall	24					
Speke	119					
Speke (West End)			264			
Stalisfield Avenue	24					
Spofforth Road	20					
Stockmoor Bungalows		14				
Townsend Avenue		36				
Towson Street	56					
Wavertree Vale	50					
Wharncliffe Road			89			

PART TWO

Belle Vale was certainly not the kind of community that well meaning experts had attempted to put into place after the war. Housing projects such as Speke and Kirkby had clearer social aims. Both were built with an idea of developing a sense of home and community by those who designed them, but it can be argued that Belle Vale succeeded where they developed problems. The reason for this is apparent when you see how the stated desires of the community were generally ignored by the experts. It is possible that not having a forced agenda meant that the Belle Vale community was allowed to develop in a way that suited the people there.

Traditional areas of tension within struggling communities were also largely avoided in the prefab estate. Joseph Williams School itself is a major example of the positive nature of the area, and significantly it welcomed both Protestant and Catholic children. It also saw many children dispersed from schools outside the area interacting with the Belle Vale kids. It became a great model for education systems of the future and later adapted to teach children with hearing difficulties.

The school and the Labour Club were very visible signs of a community developing its own rules and making them work. There were, however, many more examples of how this community grew that seem to defy expectation. Maybe you need to have been there at each stage to truly understand how it all happened. Another reason why these memories are so invaluable.

CAREFREE DAYS

"there were woods, a pathway and loads of puddles to play in"

I could probably fill a book with the adventures and misadventures we had in those days! The prefabs were still being put up and they would arrive on wagons. The parts were moved into place by small bogies running on narrow gauge rails. Each night after the men went home we would put the bogies back on the tracks and push each other around the site.

One of our more innovative ideas concerned the electrified fence across the brook from the corner of Sunnyfield Road. We would tell lads from the school that if they touched the fence with a wand they could get access to the field. We had made the wand from wire. I recall one lad from Speke called Paul McCartney who was taken in by this ruse. Possibly the start of an electrifying career!
Chuck Smith
71 Braehurst Rd

YESTERDAYS . . . Macca, fourth from left in the back row, had love not rock 'n' roll on his mind at 10. Are you or your mum or dad in our photo?

Joseph Williams school photo with Paul McCartney

Bath night. Sunday, after tea. We only had one, once a week because we had to put the immersion heater on and we had a 'shilling meter'. My mum would sit with the fellow who came to empty the meter, and most times she would get discount, and we would get a little back for sweets.
Irene Wagner nee Sudlow
61 Charlwood Road

School holidays were spent in the farm fields, building dams in `The Brook' and rafting on the various ponds in the area. Other times we would ride bikes out towards The Brickwall Pub and Cronton. Occasionally we would cross the Mersey on the old Transporter Bridge at Widnes. I think we went as far as Frodsham and Chester but can't be sure. My entire childhood memory consists of hot summers, cold winters and freedom to roam.
Eric Smith
55 Sunnyfield Road

Moving to the wonder of the countryside in Gateacre at that time, from a tenement in the Dingle, seemed like a different and exciting world to me.

That summer, being about twelve years old, I decided it was time for an adventure. A camping trip was in order. So armed with my one-man tent, a camping stove and my mam's fur coat (no sleeping bag for me), I made my way to the outback, namely The Nook to set up residence for the night on the railway embankment. Everything went along swimmingly, sausage fried, tent set up and as the evening drew in, coat on to keep warm.

Not long after bedding down, I was startled by a rustling noise and a flash light coming up the hill. I made my way warily out of the tent, trying to act a lot braver than I felt. There, making his way towards me, was a constable, beam shining ahead of him. He took one look at this hairy apparition looming at the top of the hill, turned tail, and ran for his life, not waiting to investigate whether I was man or beast. I still have a chuckle to this day over my "bear" escapade and often wonder whether he told his colleagues about the night he stumbled across wild game near the cricket field.
Tom Foster
22 Lee Park Avenue

Jim Allen age 13, 1950. New Raleigh bike. 21 Whinhurst Rd

 I remember the day of the Coronation of the Queen. Our house was the only house to have a television. One of those nine inch screen types!

My dad and mum had invited all the neighbours in to watch the ceremony and to make the day special, Dad bought cases of beer. While everybody was watching this historic programme me and my best mate Arnie Roberts nipped out into the kitchen, pinched a couple of bottles of beer and sneaked off to drink it in the bus shelter opposite the house. We had as good a time as the adults!
Jim Allen
21 Whinhurst Road

Jim was a valued member of the Belle Vale Committee until his sad death last year.

It was a cold and misty evening as we made our way along Besford Road. I must have been about eight or nine, my sister Jo being younger. There, to our amazement, lying in the middle of the road was a large Christmas tree. A gift from above. We were so excited as the three of us, Mum, Jo and I dragged it home. To us, it was the biggest and best tree we had ever seen. We even had to cut a bit off the top to fit it in the living room. We spent the whole weekend making our paper decorations and cotton wool snow for it. It really did seem an extra special Christmas that year. By the way, if anyone out there was waiting for a tree to arrive that year, that never came...sorry!

Pam Foster nee Lewis
33 Birkside Road

Pam & Joey Lewis ready to go to New Brighton, 33 Birkside Rd

In the early fifties we had a pantomime at the Community Centre. Cinderella was played by Julie Arthur and her sister Carol played Dandini. The Arthurs' uncle was Ted Ray, the famous Liverpool comedian. I think that John Leatherbarrow played Baron Hardup. Terry Mustin and I were the Ugly Sisters and I can remember we sang Diamonds are a Girl's Best Friend!
Chuck Smith

One summer's day we arrived home after a day out to find some people having a picnic in our garden. They didn't seem to think this was at all odd and it appeared to them to be the normal thing to do!
George Laurence
75 Lineside Road

Every year for our school summer holidays my sister Pam and I went to Holland to visit our family. One year, on the day before we went, I was with my friend Jillian when her next door neighbour's son came round. Jillian told him where we were going to which he replied; 'That's nothing, we're going to Talacre!' Well, as we had never heard of it, we thought it was somewhere really exotic.

It was more than twenty years later and my aunty was visiting from Holland. My husband and I were taking her sightseeing in North Wales and the penny dropped. There it was on a road sign; T-A-L-A-C-R-E. We laughed all the way home – very exotic caravan parks they have there!
Pam Foster nee Lewis

When I was very young I was rather partial to Marshmallow biscuits and the lady on groceries in the Co-op, Ivy, would always ask me several times what the biscuits I wanted were called and me thinking she was a bit deaf replied louder each time. Everyone in the shop always thought it was hilarious and I didn't know what all the fuss was about. Years later I found out that I had been asking for 'arsemellows'.
Jo Potter nee Lewis
33 Birkside Road

Linda Guy. 47 Hedgefield Rd

My childhood memories of those lazy summer days, strolling up the lanes with a bottle of water and jam butties, or broken biscuits from Irwin's, and not returning home until tea time, seem magical to me now. Who needed to go on holiday when we had all this on our doorstep? It was a shame to lose Gateacre as we knew it. Though, I suppose the people from the village thought the same when the prefabs were built and their peace became a playground for us children of the 40s.

Linda Archer nee Guy
47 Hedgefield Road

My dad was a painter and decorator who worked for McRea and Price on Halewood Road, Woolton. My mum was a housewife and as far as I can remember she never went to work while I was young. I remember playing on a lot of waste ground near the prefabs. There were woods and a pathway where we used to get to our infant school and loads of puddles to play in.

Bobby Walls
95 Charlwood Road

We always used the stile as a short cut to the farm on Grange Lane where we got eggs. We never went along the path between the two fields as it was very overgrown and full of creepy crawlies and flying things, instead we would cross the field — the one that didn't have the cows in!

Jo Potter nee Lewis

Robert Wood, 1960. 93 Sunnyfield Rd

I was born in 93, Sunnyfield Road on Easter Sunday in 1957. At the top of the road separating the prefabs from the arable farmland was a small stream known locally as the `brook'. I recall spending many hours playing alongside the brook and in particular racing sticks with Philip Pettit as we walked along the bank. I can also remember falling in on a few occasions and being told off by my mum.

Like many other young boys I was football crazy and can remember playing many enjoyable games of football in the school yard during breaks and lunchtimes. We had a school gardener, a tall thin young man who cycled to work called Bruce, who delighted in telling us off if the ball strayed on to the grassed area. I recall seeing him for many years after we left the prefabs still working as a gardener in and around the Liverpool 25 area.
Robert Wood
93 Sunnyfield Road

I have vivid memories of playing in "the woods", on the big rope swing over the "Madgie" (pond), or the other one on the big beech tree, that was the one where you could launch yourself off the top of the air-raid shelter. One of my horrible experiences was not being allowed to land back on the banks after swinging over the "Madgie". The lads kept pushing me out instead of pulling me in and I hung on to that rope for as long as I could but sadly the arms gave out in the end, bringing cheers of delight from the lads. I got a good thumping when I got home with me knickers and frock dripping wet with muddy, stagnant water.
Moira Turner nee Williamson
67 Charlwood Road

An enduring memory I have from my early life in the prefabs is the felling of the lovely tree that sat on the banks of the brook that ran along the end of our avenue. I am not sure what variety of tree it was. But I can remember it was big and beautiful. Perhaps I loved it because we did not have many mature trees at the top end of Cloverdale and it was special.

I recall as soon as we were old enough we would play down by the brook, often without permission. Lovely hot summer's days when we would find a narrow part of the brook to get over to the pond, we called Jackson's, or to play in the fields. We searched for a place, then jump. Invariably one of us would slip and a foot would slide into the water and then we would have to wait for ages for our shoes and socks to dry before we could go home.

All of these memories are focused around the tree and the wildlife that lived in and around it. We would bring home frog spawn in jars and watch for the tadpoles to hatch. It was a time of happiness and of feeling safe. I am not sure of the date that everything changed, but I recall the big machines coming and making the brook into a barren, steep-sided culvert, then the men erecting a high fence complete with barbed wire.

They cut down the tree and sawed it into tiny bits and the lovely natural habitat was destroyed. I think the destruction of the tree could be likened to the destruction of the prefabs and the unique community that existed there. Although, when I look back at the old photos it was not as big or as magnificent as I thought, but it will always stay beautiful to me.

Kathleen Corrie nee Brown
39 Cloverdale Rd

Kathleen Brown. 39 Cloverdale Rd

EVERYDAY LIFE

"a detached home, with a garden and community for our family after the war"

My prefab was the last but one avenue in Sunnyfield, on the far side of the Junior School. It was more or less opposite the boys' toilet block. There were eight houses in the avenue. Am I right in thinking that bins were collected by horse drawn wagons in those early years?

Dad always had a vegetable garden and Mum took in piecework sewing to make ends meet. Later she worked in a sweet shop in Garston and then moved to the Lybro factory on Mount Vernon.

I remember going through the Well Lane area in the dark and playing games with our torches. It was mainly farmland then. We had total freedom and nothing happened to any of us...as far as I know.

Every autumn we would join the Christmas club at the sweet shop run by a family called Begley. They lived on Childwall Valley Road. We paid pennies a week and by Christmas had enough to buy our mums a box of chocolates. There was a chandler, where we bought paraffin oil for the oil stove, firewood and Aunt Sally to clean the floors. The rest of the row had a Sayers, a butcher, Waterworth's, the greengrocers and a chippy. Bread was ten pence farthing and chips were six pence in the summer and four pence in the winter, when potatoes were cheaper. We would take old newspapers to the chippy and these were recycled as wrapping paper.

There were other shops at the top of Cloverdale. I remember only The Co-op and would often walk up there to get things for mum. I still know the dividend number.
Eric Smith

At the west end were the corporation yard where we went to report any problems with our Prefab and the storage building where we sold jam jars for recycling and bought paraffin oil. Also there were the stables which later became little stores; a greengrocer (McDonalds), a chandlers and a grocer/sweet shop. Cutting through the entry at the side you got into Charlwood Road section of the Prefabs. There was a piece of wasteland there with a dugout complete with roofs and chimneys that the local brats had built. This piece of land became the scout hut where we built a concrete prefab building.

Dennis Partington
Birkside Road

The Rag & Bone Man used to come round and if you had anything for him he would give you a plate or a goldfish. I asked one day if we could have a goldfish, but unfortunately it didn't last very long!

Janet Lansdowne nee Laurence
75 Lineside Road

The origins of Belle Vale Chapel were in Garston Gospel Hall in Long Lane. One of their members, Bill Allen, lived in the prefabs with his wife, Lena and son, John. In the 1950's he began a Sunday school, which was eventually held in Belle Vale County Primary School. Children from the Sunday School were able to go to the Merseyside Christian Youth Camps in North Wales, which are still functioning today. I particularly remember attending a Billy Graham meeting at Manchester where I received an assurance of my faith.

At first Sunday services were held in a scout hut, but eventually a permanent chapel was built in Lineside Road in 1966.

Perhaps I had to reach the age of sixty before I could fully understand the way God went ahead of me. He provided a detached home, with a garden and community for our family after the war. There were good schools for us, and activities for young and old organised by public-spirited citizens.

Sue Wilding nee Benson
42 Whinhurst Road

Many of us went to Sunday School at the Salvation Army. I think it was known as Belle Vale Home Corps and was held in Joseph Williams. I loved Sgt. Major Howarth and his wife who worked so hard for us, and also little Brother Jones who came with us for our yearly outing. We'd all climb on the charas in Sunnyfield and head off to Helsby Hill. It seemed to take forever to get there and when we got to Ditton we'd all hold our noses because of the chemical smell! We knew it wasn't too far from "Dirty Ditton" to Helsby where we ran races and had tea in a big hut.

There was an annual prize giving at Sunday School for good attendance. Billy Liddell presented me with a Bible one year and signed it for me. I still have it and also another book.

Dot James nee Maddox
63 Sunnyfield Road

Dot Maddox - Bible autographed by Billy Liddell

As a keen naturalist I used to like to take the opportunity of taking the class out of school to look at the countryside. There was lots of countryside to explore; ponds to dip, wild flowers to identify, trees, hedges, birds, creepy crawlies — lots to look at. One of these weeks we went along a farm track past Cockshead Farm. On an impulse I found an old plank of wood and with a piece of chalk printed the name `Cockshead Road'. I don't really think I influenced the City Planners, but it's nice idea!
Donald Headey

The farm track referred to now forms part of Cockshead Road! Over the years there has been some variation in the spelling of the name of the farm.

School Nature Walk 1956

Coxhead Farm Nature Walk. Belle Vale School, 1956

One of the most lasting memories is my involvement with the 5th Childwall Cub pack, run by Eric Smith, which operated out of a purpose built hut. This hut was located on the site which now houses Morrison's. The time and energy put into this cub pack by Eric Smith and his team of supporters helped many young boys from the prefabs to avail themselves of opportunities that I am sure they would not have found if this wonderful community service had not been provided.
Robert Wood

Sandra Ward. 15 Besford Rd

Pat Sharp was the leader of the Morris Dancing. She was thirteen but was so tall. I was the mascot aged about 5 years. I was in the two troops but left Belle Vale Troop to go to Morris Dancing with my friend Sandra Torres in Norris Green. We would go and practise on a Friday sometimes and stay over at Sandra Torres's Grandma's so that we could go Morris Dancing to the Saturday carnivals all over the North West and North Wales, parading through the streets to; "She wore a teeny weeny yellow polka dot bikini".
Sandra Sandland nee Ward
15 Besford Road

My dad was a keen gardener and was the proud owner of a greenhouse and a member of a gardening club where they called him Tonks, because he used to go on about Tonks Manure.
Ted Fish
17 Sunnyfield Road

Thinking back now, I feel very lucky to have had my childhood in the prefabs. It was a close community, children could play outside, `on the end' under the lamp in the winter, in and out of gardens playing Hide and Seek and, more importantly, in safety.

Great place for parties as well. We had our Coronation Party in the avenue. All the houses were decorated and a good time was had by all! It is a long time ago, but I remember all the mothers contributing food etc. for the big day. All the children were given Coronation Mugs. Ours were in mum's house and unfortunately I broke ours quite recently! Community was very important. Dad was in the Gardening Club. All of the gardens were looked after. Maybe people like us had come from houses without gardens so took particular pride in the outside of the houses.
Margaret Cannon nee McDonald
99 Besford Road

Besford Road Neighbours Coronation Party

Hilda & Phil Young with son Phil, 1965. 41 Bridgefield Rd

My family moved to the Belle Vale prefab estate from the centre of Liverpool in 1947. It was the century's coldest winter and together with the prefab's reputation for being cold and damp the move could be likened to a life sentence in Siberia.

My family's new domestic arrangements were not helped by the weekly jibe on radio's Charlie Chester show, "Down in the jungle living in a tent better than a prefab...no rent."

However we did have an "American style kitchen" and we were able to make our own lolly ices, though demand during that ice cold winter of '47 was somewhat limited.

The estate did not have a school. Not until 1950 when Joseph Williams Primary opened... named after the Alderman who was Liverpool Corporation's director of Education.

Although the school was in the middle of an estate, it was a short distance from the farms, woods and streams that made up the area between Liverpool's boundary and Tarbock and Huyton in those far off days.

"Pop" Gore was the ideal headmaster of the school. He was prone to interrupt the normal curriculum of the class...and we would suddenly find ourselves on an impromptu nature walk, spotting rabbits and grass snakes and being given a detailed account of the flora near to the school.

It was into this gentle academic world one Monday morning that two green double decker Corpy buses arrived at the school gates. The buses were full...bringing "overspill" pupils from Stockton Wood school in Speke, the biggest primary school in England but unable to cope with the burgeoning post war baby boom taking place in its catchment area.

Several of the Speke overspill pupils joined my class...including a cherubic lad destined to challenge as a teacher's pet not something that endeared him to non contenders such as myself. His name was Paul McCartney and he was one of a pair...his younger brother Michael joining another class.

Paul and I left Joseph Williams in 1953.... the year of the Coronation.... Edmund Hillary and Sherpa Tensing conquering Everest...the Stanley Matthews Cup Final. We left behind the gentle leadership of Pop Gore for the more formidable reputations of J.R. Edwards at the Liverpool Institute and A.G. Russell at the Holt.
Phil Young
41 Bridgefield Road

TOUGH TIMES

"you woke to ice on the inside of the bedroom windows"

Our prefab was scrubbed clean, bleached and polished inside and out on a regular basis. Mum's standards of cleanliness were very high and we (my three sisters and I) all had jobs to do each Saturday while Mum was at work. Dad would join in too if he was home, but he mainly helped on Sundays; peeling veg, cooking dinner, washing up and setting our small fire. There are memories of watching the orange reflection from this fire dancing on the walls whilst waiting for the 'grub up, tea's ready' call form the kitchen.

Afterwards we had clean cotton sheets warmed by hot water bottles. Then we lay in bed watching the patterns from the paraffin heater dancing on the ceiling.

Outside our house was a coal shed. Each prefab had one made of corrugated iron built into an arch with a brick wall at the back and a wooden door at the front. In ours the coal was kept at the back and two small benches either side in front. When we were small we would sometimes sit in there in awe of the dark silence and watch the dust dancing in the shafts of light which came in through holes in the iron. If you put your fingers up to the light you could see through your skin blood and sinews, not for the squeamish.

Behind the shed was a compost heap where we grew the best fruit laden blackcurrant bush you have ever seen. From this we made jam and pies and the best fruit lolly ices ever. We also made rhubarb lollies and pies. Apart from this and the occasional old rose bush our large prefab garden was a mess! Wild, overgrown, it was a monument to the old slash and burn system of agriculture, the only one in existence outside of Asia as far as I know.

Gladys Williams
Lineside Road

It was early January 1963 and I had just come home from having my son James by Caesarean Section. I had just taken my daughters Carol and Bernadette out of the bath when a lorry came crashing into our Prefab, crushing half of it. The driver had crashed into cars and came down the embankment before crashing into our prefab. We were all very lucky to be alive.

Emily Fullan
138 Whinhurst Road

I always remember playing 'split the kipper' (you stand, legs apart, while someone throws a knife between them) with John Murphy, and the knife split my hand, flew into my left eye and blinded me. We had to go to one of the houses to telephone an ambulance to come and take me to hospital

We used to go looking for eggs in Charlwood Woods. I remember going under the tunnel going towards Grange Lane. On the farm there, on the left hand side up the little lane, was a yacht, and we all used to think it was Noah's Ark. We got into a bit of trouble with the farmer there. Me and another boy were in his orchard, he caught us and whacked me with the big stick he carried.

When me mum was short of coal we used to go to the railway line and when the trains were passing throw stones at the driver and he would throw lumps of coal back at us!

I always remember going in Bowles sweet shop and finding a 10 bob note and not knowing what it was. Me dad conned me when he said "Oh that's a doctors note. Give it to me", and he gave me 2 bob for it.
Frank Lawrence
8 Charlwood Road

Brian, Frank & Ken Lawrence. 8 Charlwood Rd

Perhaps the cold winters are the stronger weather memories. The prefabs were freezing and you woke to ice on the inside of the bedroom windows. You dragged your clothes into the bed, waited for them to warm and pulled them on...who needed a daily shower! A once a week bath was enough.

The electricity often failed in the early years. We had an oil stove in the kitchen...often the only warm room, and mum would warm the cornflake milk on it.
Eric Smith

Margaret Rycraft, proud owner of 2nd hand bike. 39 Birkside Rd

The coal fire in the prefab heated the water. If no water was used it became hot. Very hot! On one occasion, as a child, I was left in the house on my own. The fire roared away for some time before I noticed some odd noises. I hadn't the faintest idea what was causing the sounds and was scared to death. I always had a vivid imagination.

When I could stand it no longer I fled to one of the neighbour's houses. Our very kind neighbour returned to the prefab with me and listened carefully. It turned out that the hot water was actually boiling in the tank. The hot tap in the kitchen was turned on, releasing some of the scalding water and thereby sorting the problem.
Margaret Hyland nee Rycraft
39 Birkside Road

I remember one woman bought a single tub Hoover washing machine and wheeled it around in a pram for anyone who wanted to borrow it for 2/6d a time. You were lucky to have it at the weekend because you had it longer.
Joan Luxon

The prefabs had quite large gardens, but the avenues were only three paving slabs wide from fence to fence. When it snowed we used to put ashes on the pavement to stop people slipping on the ice. The bedrooms were that cold we used to have icicles hanging from the window sills inside, and the windows were always thick with ice. The coal sheds were actually Anderson shelters. We used to sit in them eating Oxo cubes.
Taylor Family

The Mowat Family
Eric, David, Eileen, Sheila at the back with baby Paul in front of her, Isabella far right

On one occasion, I really contravened the health and safety laws and went near the railway line. Marie Moore from up the street had been on the railway line a few weeks earlier and had been hit by a train. I don't know how, but she got away with just a broken arm.

All the kids in the neighbourhood were severely warned after that accident not to go anywhere near the trains. What etched into my memory was not so much that incident itself but the beating I got with the hose pipe off the washing machine when I had been caught on the railway embankment. Being at least fifteen yards from the line didn't count in parents' eyes, I had strayed across the fence and that was enough. If the trains couldn't get me, my mother would.

I remember my sister shouting, "Mother, Mother. Stop it. You'll kill her," but I honestly don't remember it hurting and that is how tough it was. I was always in trouble for giving cheek or something and fighting with the lads was nothing new. Once some lad (who shall be nameless, but you know who you are!) wound me up so much I think he was being insulting or something so I punched him right on the nose and blood came spurting out, much to my shock and amazement.On winter nights we used to play hedge hopping which involved running across as many gardens as we could, like escapees from prison or SAS men without being caught. When we occasionally did disturb the occupant of a prefab we would lie low as light from the open door shone across the garden. There were plenty of hedges and bushes to hide beneath. (The smell of damp earth always reminds me of these adventures.) Like all good SAS men we learned not to breathe on these occasions until our would - be captors had given up and gone back inside to watch telly. We were good and never got caught.

Of course there was that caring old stand by, knock and run. It must have annoyed the neighbours so much to have to get up and answer the door. Watching at a distance at their perplexed or annoyed expressions was always good for a laugh. How childish we all were... but then again I suppose we were only kids.
Gladys Williams

Jimmy Moore's story of the rail incident - Marie is his little sister - is on p68 of "Prefab Days"

When I was about five or six years old, my older brother Chuck and I were in the bathroom. He told me to stand in the sink. There was a mirror over the sink to shave and also a light fitting. He told me to put my finger in the light fitting. As I did, he pulled the cord and I got such a shock. Eventually my nail went black and fell off. I never did it again!
John Smith
71 Braehurst Road

Brian & Jenny Gwilt on their wedding Day. 42 Endbrook Rd

I remember one night when our kitchen was so full of friends that Diane Pemberton decided to sit on the wash boiler next to the cooker. Very full skirts were all the rage at the time and I think she wanted to show off her frilly underskirt. Unfortunately she did not realize that the cooker was still hot. Her skirt caught fire, she was promptly dunked into the adjacent sink and the taps switched on. Luckily, she was not hurt, but her skirt did not fair too well!
Jenny Gwilt nee Steele
Braehurst Road

The Roberts family had an old Bakelite radio which began to give off an awful smell when switched on. It transpired that a tiny mouse had got into it and had been electrocuted. Every time the radio was switched on the mouse `warmed up' and stank!
Ruth Roberts nee Otterson

My friend, who was six months older than me and working, talked me into going as a film extra on 'Ferry Across the Mersey'. I sneaked off school undetected, I thought, only to find myself in a front-page photo in the Echo! Needless to say my Mum wasn't too pleased. Worse still, they'd cut my appearance out of the film!
Jo Potter nee Lewis

Tinder Box Play 1954 Belle Vale School. Jimmy Moore 8th from left

In those days we had to make our own fun and so I used to have a wheel and stick, no tyre on the wheel, just a bike wheel. I wouldn't go anywhere without it, it was like a car to me. If anyone wanted anything from the shops, I used to go but I had to take my wheel and stick with me or I wouldn't go. One day I went on a message for one of the neighbours up to Stellamore Road and I "parked" my wheel and my stick outside Stellamore shops. When I came out my wheel and stick had been robbed. I was in a depression for quite a while, and I wouldn't go out or anything. One day my Mum called me out and said there was someone to see me. There was some man standing there and he said, 'I believe you had your wheel robbed'. I said yes and he gave me a brand new wheel with a blown up tyre and a new stick. Well, I was over the moon and I went out after that.
Jimmy Moore
118 Lineside Road

I still remember the great time we had digging caves in the brook that ran behind our house and the times 'Old Farmer Rimmer' tried to give us some of his buckshot for being in his field.
Peter Cowperthwaite
Cloverdale Road

I went to Joseph Williams and actually sat next to Paul McCartney. He was horrible to me. He used to pull my hair and pinch me. I was glad when he left.
Taylor Family

Edna Latta, 17yrs. 103 Sunnyfield Rd

In 1954 my mother died and my sister and I had to give up the prefab, because we were too young to keep the house on. So my sister went to live with my Auntie in Kirkby and I went to a home in Upper Parliament Street in Liverpool.

I was there five years. I was only eighteen when I went in there and the oldest person was 90 years old. I got spoilt and got called the baby. I had my 21st birthday there. I had 72 birthday cards and three birthday cakes. A few weeks later Frankie Vaughan the singer came to see me. He stayed for about an hour. He was appearing at the Empire. I went and saw him with my sister and one of the nurses.

I moved to another home called Angers House, which was for cerebral palsy people and they were all my age. We used to have some good times. I was there nine years and then I came and went to a Leonard Cheshire Home in Woolton. It is quite nice. I have my own bedroom and my own things. I go out quite a lot. My family comes twice a week.

Edna Latta
103 Sunnyfield Road

I used to love going to Our Lady of the Assumption School Youth Club, which had its dance on a Thursday. I used to love jiving with my flowered skirt with net and hook petticoats underneath, which, when you sat down, you had to hold the skirt down.

At around this time there were gangs of Teddy Boys. I remember coming home from Our Lady's youth club on a foggy night. My friend and I were crossing over Belle Vale Road when we were confronted by a line of Teddy Boys with chains. They scared the life out of us.

Sandra Blyth nee Cheverton
103 Sunnyfield Road

Early in the fifties my husband Gerry took very ill with TB Meningitis. He was operated on in the Neurosurgical Unit in Walton Hospital. A member of the medical team was a Dr Charles Evans.

One day, when I visited Gerry, he told me Dr. Charles had been to say goodbye to him as he was going off to climb Everest, not realising the significance of that. It was quite a surprise when it was announced on Coronation Day that a team had successfully reached the top of Mount Everest and one of the members was Dr. Charles Evans. I understand he, along with one other, were the first to attempt to reach the top but as they were nearing it they discovered there was something wrong with the oxygen and decided they would reach the top but would not return, so they turned back.

That is when Hillary and Tensing took over and, as they say, the rest is an important part of our history. Dr. Charles, in our minds, was a member of two very successful teams! He later became a Professor at Aberystwyth University where I had been evacuated during the war. Another member of the medical team was a sister in law of Miss Clothier who taught at Our Lady's Junior School.

Having seen how much Gerry suffered with the TB I decided to help in the Campaign to encourage the inoculation against it, namely BCG, by volunteering to go door to door in a section of Charlwood Road. Thankfully it was successful.

Joan Luxon

We had originally set a date of March 1965 to get married, but Bill's company asked him to work on a contract in Suffolk for two years. That seemed a long time to be apart when you were young and in love.

On a visit home in May 1964 we decided to bring the wedding forward, so that I would be able to go to Suffolk with Bill. We set the date of 25th July with Mr Siviter, the vicar of St. Stephen's church, and also arranged the wedding cars, but couldn't find a venue for the reception with such short notice [six weeks].

The reception had to be held in our prefab. A neighbour that didn't have any children said we could store the furniture and carpet from the living room in their spare bedroom. This was done on the Friday evening before the wedding. Mum worked in Joseph Williams School so she arranged to borrow some trestle tables chairs and benches from the canteen.

The living room was set up to accommodate twenty guests for the wedding reception. Two of Mum's friends waited on the tables. After the meal the tables were cleared away and the chairs and benches put up against the walls, and the room made ready to welcome more guests to the evening reception. They did manage to spill over into the kitchen, hall and out into the garden as the evening went on, but everyone said they had a good time.

Sandra Harrison nee Wood and Bill Harrison
93 Sunnyfield Road

Sandra Wood marries Bill Harrison 1964. 93 Sunnyfield Rd

21 Besford Rd 1948-49

Jackson's Pond

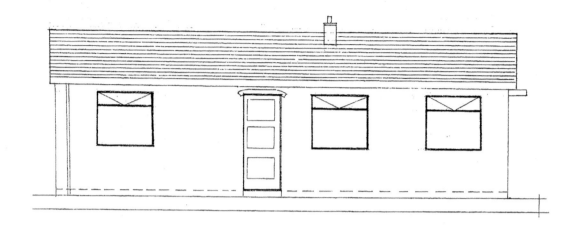

<u>FRONT VIEW</u>

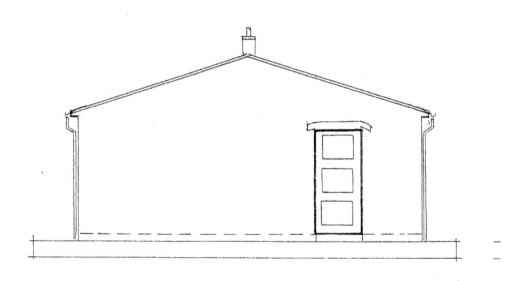

<u>END VIEW</u>

Thanks to Harry Ro

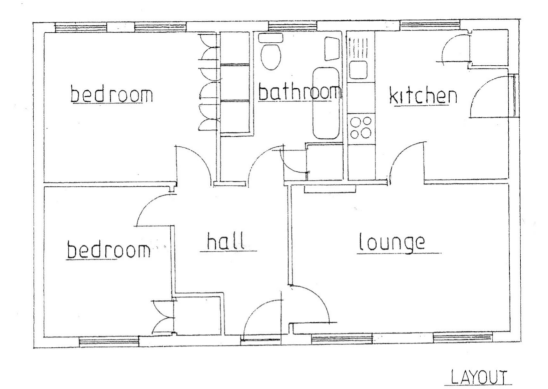

bedroom   bathroom   kitchen

bedroom   hall   lounge

LAYOUT

REAR VIEW

PART THREE

Despite the cold, the bedding in problems and the dangers of the countryside, Belle Vale estate had looked like an indestructible community. But it was destined to be destroyed.

We have tried to discover discussions on how this community could be kept going, but found little. It appears that a government free from the crises left by the war is less likely to adapt to circumstance. In fact it seems totally unwilling to do so. The area had always been earmarked for a very different type of housing development. When and how this happened seemed the only issues left. Private industry was to have a bigger say, and changes were going to evolve around developer's needs. It was obvious that a self sufficient community were far from being part of this.

There is always more to find out. What exactly happened to all the Belle Vale homes? Do any still exist in museums or as privately owned curiosities? It would be nice to talk to someone involved in the construction of the Belle Vale prefab. Are there people from other prefab estates with very different experiences from those within these books?

The memories provided over the two publications have been very important for those who were there. They have also inspired many other people to think about how their lives can be fuller and have the same sense of belonging that is rich within these pages. Everyone involved should be proud of that.

FAREWELL TO THE PREFABS

"it was loaded onto a lorry and maybe reborn as a holiday home"

Stephen Woods blowing bubbles, 1963. 31 Cloverdale Rd

The day came when we were going to leave our prefab. There was a sense of security about our little home as most things were done for us if anything went wrong. In our case we bought a house in Score Lane, Childwall where everything had to be done by the owner - and paid for!
G E Benstead
2 Besford Road

We moved out of our Prefab in April 1957. As we were getting ready to leave a gypsy with a horse and cart came round and took away everything we didn't want.
George Laurence
75 Lineside Road

I remember going back after we had left the prefabs to see our house lying flat on the ground and learning that night it was loaded by some men onto a low loader lorry and maybe reborn as a holiday home.
Stephen Woods
31 Cloverdale Road

I don't remember the date we left the prefabs and moved to Deepdale Road but I do recall my dad dug up his privet hedge. He got Freddie Prothero to carry it to the new house on his moped, causing a great deal of hilarity in the neighbourhood!
Chuck Smith

When the prefabs were being demolished Jack Williams used to go and get the doors to make a shed. A friend told him one was empty, so he goes along. Then, when he went to take the last one, the kitchen door, he got a shock. There were veg cooking on the kitchen cooker! He did a hasty retreat and never found out who lived there!
Nellie Crookham, 103 Charlwood Road

Nellie Crookham, 103 Charlwood Road

I was nine years old when we left the prefabs for our new council house in Halewood. We still lived in the prefabs when Everton beat Manchester United 1- 0 in the semi final of the FA Cup, but I recall watching the final, 14th May 1966 on TV in our house in Halewood.

The move to Halewood was not a success and although I made new friends my Mum never settled and yearned for the prefabs and the Belle Vale area.
On my route to school from Lee Park I watched the final demise of the prefabs as one by one they fell to the demolishers.
Robert Wood

When we were being moved from Everton to the prefab, my dad made the comment that he didn't want to go and live in a corrugated iron shed. After three of the happiest and most memorable years we left, and he cried because he didn't want to.
Diane Allen nee Christian
74 Charlwood Road

HOMES SMASHED UP
BUT THEIR SPIRIT LINGERS ON

"you had to be tough to stay when yours was the only prefab left on the block"

The text that follows is from a beautiful but uncredited piece from The Liverpool Weekly News in August 1968. We have made all efforts possible to track down the author but could not do so by the time of going to press. If anyone has any details about the author please get in touch.

To many people, "prefab" is a dirty word - a polite term for something approaching a slum. But the old prefab estate in Belle Vale housed one of the closest and finest communities Liverpool will ever see.

Of several hundred prefabs covering an 80-acre strip of land alongside Childwall Valley Road, only two remain. The rest have been left for vandals to smash up and workmen to demolish.

But it was not always like that, I lived on the estate for nearly 20 years, and I remember it as a tightly knit community, the homes surrounded by corn fields and scattered farm houses. Buses served the estate once every hour, and the giant brick estates of Lee Park and Childwall Valley were still on the drawing board.

The prefabs themselves boasted neat, well-kept gardens, a kitchen, bathroom, two bedrooms, a hall and living room and community-conscious families.

Their story begins at the end of the last war. When the prefabs were first erected – as "temporary accommodation"- they formed the largest prefabricated estate in Britain. Many of them were occupied by ex-servicemen and their families, but people from many other walks of life contributed to the community.

ISOLATION
Whether it was a sense of isolation – the nearest place of any status being old Gateacre Village – or whether the people were just naturally friendly, the result was a close community feeling which developed into a kind of resentment of outside

interference. When the large new estate at Lee Park came along it brought the first signs of change. The bus service was increased to every few minutes and the prefab dwellers found themselves surrounded by more and more people.

Most of the prefab people had forgotten the Corporation's promise that the prefabs would be up for ten years at the most. There was no sign of the prefabs coming down and they were regarded as homes for life by many of the older people.

Then came the next big change. Right opposite to where I was living, over the other side of Childwall Valley Road, bulldozers began to turn the farmland into foundations for brick houses and eleven-storey flats.

The character of the area changed completely. The bus service was improved still further to one bus every seven minutes. Shops were built on the new Childwall Valley estate which already claimed at least half a dozen sky-scraper blocks.

THE "CHIPPY"

The small grocery shop a hundred yards from my home at the top of Whinhurst Road was converted into a fish and chip shop. At first, the 'chippy' was a novelty – the first time that end of the prefab estate had ever had one. But when gangs, said to come from the neighbouring new estates, began to loiter in the area and leave chip papers in prefab gardens, the novelty wore off.

But even the large majority of the prefab people had no thought of moving home. Although it was 18 years since the prefabs had been built – eight years longer than the ten year maximum life promised by the Corporation – the thought of moving was pushed to the back of the minds of most people.

Then suddenly the jolt came. Letters from the corporation said that plans were under way to clear the way and build on the land. Immediately there was uproar. Apart from a few families, who were willing to go, the whole of the prefab estate said they would refuse to move. So strong was the community feeling that in spite of the fact that the nearby new estates had altered the area, there was talk of barricading doors and windows if the Corporation tried to force a move.

Other prefab-dwellers asked why their homes couldn't be bricked off by putting permanent brick walls around the prefabs and turning them into proper bungalows.

"TOP MEN"

Tenants committees were formed, meetings were held, "top men" from the Council and Corporation came down to the estate to make the prefab people "see reason".

Then it was discovered that a new estate was planned for Naylors Road and Netherley Road, which skirted the prefab estate on its western side. So the prefab families asked if they could all be moved together to the new estate and stay in the area. Why this plan never worked no-one seems to know. Instead offers were made to individual families in various parts of the prefab estate, and this seems to be what broke the back of resistance.

The prefabs were laid out in small avenues with six homes each. Instead of beginning at one end of the estate and moving people together, empty prefabs began to appear in isolated parts of the estate. The vacated prefabs looked like they had been hit by a bomb. No-one wanted to live next to anything like that, and so people began to take the first offers of accommodation that came along.

A few families stuck it out and eventually moved to Nayorsfield – the new estate which is still being built close to the site of the prefab estate.

But you had to be tough to stay when yours was the only prefab left out of half a dozen on the block. Minutes after a prefab was vacated children from other areas would smash every window in the place, force the doors open, smash what they could inside and then set fire to the lot.

Shouting at them got you nowhere. Police at the new station at Belle Vale were co-operative, but pointed out that it was a big job when there was an average of two fires every night

DROPPED

One of the first places to feel the effects of the moves was the local school - Joseph Williams County Primary School. Its total of 500 pupils dropped to 180 in a very short time.

Most children on the prefab estate, both Catholic and Protestant, went to the school at some time during their lives. Although it was some time ago since I was taught there I remember it as one of the cleanest and best cared for school buildings in Liverpool. And when I returned there to look at the old prefab estate as it is now I found the school still laid claim to the same clean look and active educational programme.

Headmaster Mr F.G.Wallard, who lives at 16 Hilltop Road, Childwall, told me; "With the people in the prefabs having to move out and the new estate at Naylorsfield about to start, I would have thought there was a golden opportunity to move the community 'en bloc'. I think the people in the prefabs would have been glad to stick it out and wait if a promise had been given them that they could all move to Naylorsfield together.

"Instead of the close community staying together, however, some went out to Halewood, others to Cantril Farm, and a few went into private property. The community was broken up, children's education was disrupted, and this marvellous chance was missed."

But Mr Wallard added that the prospects for Joseph Williams School were good. "Although the number of pupils dropped sharply," he said. "It has now begun to pick up again with children moving into the Naylorsfield estate from other parts of the city. By the end of September this year I think we should see the number up to about 300."

Close to the school is one of the two remaining prefabs on the estate. I talked to the people living there, Mr. And Mrs. Bill Pinnington.

The Pinningtons have been in the story from the beginning – they moved into the prefab at 175 Cloverdale Road when the prefabs themselves were only just being built. As they jokingly put it; "We were first in and last out."

QUITE HAPPY

Mr Pinnington still keeps his garden properly. He said; "People come here and see the overgrown weeds and hedges round about and they ask me why I bother keeping our garden tidy. They don't seem to realise that we are still living here. As long as we are here we are going to keep it as a home should be kept – and that includes the garden."

And 51-year-old Mr. Pinnington added, "As far as my wife and I are concerned we are quite happy to stay here even now. We don't want to move at all – it's nice and quiet with nobody around and we just happen to like our prefab."

But like the hundreds of other families who once lived on the estate, the Pinningtons are going to have to go. They told me they expected about two weeks longer in the prefab before they were given an offer of alternative accommodation which they could not sensibly refuse.

WEEDS

To look at the prefab sites now you would never think the area was once as the Pinningtons and many other families remember it.

Instead of the cornfields and the stream nearby there are new housing estates, new roads, and different people. Thistles and woods have sprung up and covered the once closely-cropped prefab lawns. Neatly trimmed hedges have doubled their size.

From the Pinningtons' home I walked up the road to where my own prefab used to be, close to the old Territorial Army barracks. The foundations can still be seen, but the garden is covered with weeds, thistles and old bricks. An old fireplace, looking very much the worse for wear, is still in its place near the centre of where the prefab used to be.

But the woods and thistles won't be there very much longer. I talked to one of the men working for the City Planning Office about plans for the site of the demolished prefab estate.

He told me that big plans have already been laid. The whole demolished area along the side of Childwall Valley Road is to be cleared and developed with more than 2,000 dwellings.

STRIKING

Through the centre of the new development will run a kind of 'spine' with two rows of dwelling, one of four storeys and one of six storeys. Beneath it will be car parking and probably private open space.

To either side of the spine will be single storey, two storey and a few three storey homes, and the whole estate will be on the traffic-free system. Pedestrians will as far as possible be kept away from roads. One striking point is that skyscraper blocks are not marked in the plan – the new estate will not be developed with this kind of dwelling.

Joseph Williams School, I was told, is about the only one of the older buildings which is being left alone. In fact, it will probably benefit from the redevelopment by being given a slice of land to use as playing fields.

The new area will have a "local centre", as planners have called the proposed development for the centre of the estate. It will include a supermarket, a civic laundry, community building and other facilities.

The whole development, which will be "home" to about 6,500 people, will supplement the large "district centre" on the other side of Childwall Valley Road, where prefabs in the other separate section are still standing. The district centre will cater for everything from shopping to entertainment, and it will be the first of about ten district centres planned for the entire city.

The Belle Vale District Centre is very much a thing of the future, but the million pound housing development on the new demolished prefab estate could begin quite soon.

How soon is difficult to say, but optimists say a start could be made by the end of the year. The main difficulty is bringing down the cost of the scheme to a figure which is acceptable to the Government. Until then the old prefab sites are likely to remain a tangle of weeds and broken bricks.

THE PREFAB PEOPLE

Homes smashed up but their spirit lingers on

BY A STAFF REPORTER

TO MANY people, "prefab" is a dirty word — a polite term for something approaching a slum. But the old prefab estate in Belle Vale housed one of the closest and finest communities Liverpool will ever see.

Of several hundred prefabs covering an 80-acre strip of land alongside Childwall Valley Road, only two remain. The rest have been left for vandals to smash up and workmen to demolish.

But it was not always like that. I lived on the estate for nearly 20 years, and I remember it as a tightly-knit community, the homes surrounded by corn fields and scattered farm houses. Buses served the estate once every hour, and the giant brick estates of Lee Park and Childwall Valley were still on the drawing board.

Mr. Bill Pinnington with his wife, Dorothy, his married daughter Sandra, and grandchildren.

The prefabs themselves boasted neat, well-kept gardens, a kitchen, bathroom, two bedrooms, a hall and living room, and community-conscious families.

Their story begins at the end of the last war. When the prefabs were first erected — as "temporary" accommodation — they formed the largest prefabricated estate in Britain. Many of them were occupied by ex-servicemen and their families, but people from many other walks of life contributed to the community.

ISOLATION

Whether it was a sense of isolation — the nearest place of any status being old Gateacre Village — or whether the people were just naturally friendly, the result was a close community feeling which developed almost into a kind of resentment of outside interference.

When the large new estate at Lee Park came along, it brought the first signs of change. The bus service was increased to every few minutes and the prefab-dwellers found themselves surrounded by more and more people.

Most of the prefab people had forgotten the Corporation's promise that the prefabs would be up for ten years at the most. There was no sign of the prefabs coming down and they were regarded as homes for life by many of the older people.

Then came the next big change. Right oposite to where I was living, over on the other side of Childwall Valley Road, bulldozers began to turn the farmland into foundations for brick houses and eleven-storey flats.

The character of the area changed completely. The bus service was improved still further to one bus every seven minutes. Shops were built on the new Childwall Valley estate, which already claimed at least half a dozen sky-scraper blocks.

THE "CHIPPY"

The small grocery shop a hundred yards from my home at the top of Winhurst Road was converted into a fish and chip shop. At first, the 'chippy' was a novelty — the first time that end of the prefab estate had ever had one. But when gangs, said to come from the neighbouring new estates, began to loiter in the area and leave chip papers in prefab gardens, the novelty wore off.

But even then, the large majority of the prefab people had no thought of moving home. Although it was 18 years since the prefabs had been built — eight years longer than the ten-year maximum life promised by the Corporation — the thought of moving was pushed to the back of the minds of most people.

Then, suddenly, the jolt came. Letters from the Corporation said that plans were under way to clear the prefabs and build on the land. Immediately there was uproar. Apart from a few families who were willing to go, the whole of the prefab estate said they would refuse to move. So strong was the community feeling that, in spite of the fact that the nearby new estates had altered the area, there was talk of barricading doors and windows if the Corporation tried to force a move.

Other prefab-dwellers asked why their homes couldn't be "bricked off" by putting permanent brick walls around the prefabs and turning them into proper bungalows.

"TOP MEN"

Tenants committees were formed, meetings were held, "top men" from the Council and Corporation came down to the estate to make the prefab people "see reason."

Then it was discovered that a new estate was planned for Naylors Road and Netherley Road, which skirted the prefab estate on its western side. So the prefab families asked if they could all be moved together to the new estate and stay in the area.

Why this plan never worked, no-one seems to know. Instead, offers were made to individual families in various parts of the prefab estate, and this seems to be what broke the back of resistance.

The prefabs were laid out in small avenues, with six homes each. Instead of beginning at one end of the estate and moving people together, empty prefabs began to appear in isolated parts of the estate, empty prefabs had done their work, the vacated prefabs looked as if they had been hit by a bomb. No-one wanted to live next to anything like that, and so people began to take the first offers of accommodation that came along.

A few families stuck it out and eventually moved to Naylorsfield — the new estate which is still being built close to the site of the prefab estate.

But you had to be tough to stay, when yours was the only prefab left out of half-a-dozen in the block. Minutes after a prefab was vacated, children from other areas would smash every window in the place, force the doors open, smash what they could inside, and then set fire to the lot.

Shouting at them got you nowhere. Police at the new station at Belle Vale were co-operative, but pointed out that it was a big job when there was an average of two fires every night.

DROPPED

One of the first places to feel the effects of the moves was the local school — Joseph Williams County Primary School. It's total of 500 pupils dropped to 180 in a very short time.

Most children on the prefab estate, both Catholic and Protestant, went to the school at some time during their lives. Although it was some time ago when I was taught there, I remember it as one of the cleanest and best cared for school buildings in Liverpool. And when I returned there to look at the old prefab estate as it is now, I found the school still laid claim to the same clean look and active educational programme.

Headmaster Mr. F. G. Wallard, who lives at 16 Hilltop Road, Childwall, told me: "With the people in the prefabs having to move out and the new estate at Naylorsfield about to start, I would have thought that here was a golden opportunity for the planners to move the community 'en bloc.' I think the people in the prefabs would have been glad to stick it out and wait if a promise had been given them that they could all move to Naylorsfield together.

"Instead of the close community staying together, however, some went out to Halewood, others to Cantril Farm, and a few went into private property. The community was broken up, children's education was disrupted, and this marvellous chance was missed."

But Mr. Wallard added that the prospects for Joseph Williams School were good. "Although the number of pupils dropped sharply," he said, "it has now begun to pick up again with children moving into the Naylorsfield estate from other parts of the city. By the end of September this year I think we should see the number up to about 300."

Close to the school is one of the two remaining prefabs on the estate. I talked to the people living there, Mr. and Mrs. Bill Pinnington.

The Pinningtons have been in the story from the beginning — they moved into the prefab at 175 Cloverdale Road when the prefabs themselves were only just being built. As they jokingly put it: "We were first in and last out."

QUITE HAPPY

Mr. Pinnington still keeps his garden properly. He said: "People come here and see the overgrown weeds and hedges round about and they ask me why I bother keeping our garden tidy. They don't seem to realise that we are still living here. As long as we are here we are going to keep it as a home should be kept — and that includes the garden."

And 51-year-old Mr. Pinnington added: "As far as my wife and I are concerned, we are quite happy to stay here even now. We don't want to move at all — it's nice and quiet with nobody around and we just happen to like our prefab."

But, like the hundreds of other families who once lived on the estate, the Pinningtons are going to have to go. They told me they expected about two weeks longer in the prefab before they were given an offer of alternative accommodation which they could not sensibly refuse.

WEEDS

To look at the prefab sites now, you would never think the area was once as the Pinningtons and many other families remember it.

Instead of the cornfields and the stream nearby, there are new housing estates, new roads, and different people. Thistles and weeds have sprung up and covered the once closely-cropped prefab lawns. Neatly trimmed hedges have doubled their size.

From the Pinnington's home I walked up the road to where my own prefab used to be, close to the old Territorial Army barracks. The foundations can still be seen, but the garden is covered with weeds, thistles and old bricks. An old fireplace, looking very much the worse for wear, is still in its place near the centre of where the prefab used to be.

But the weeds and thistles won't be there for very much longer. I talked to one of the men working for the City Planning Officer about plans for the site of the demolished prefab estate.

He told me that big plans have already been laid. The whole demolished area along the side of Childwall Valley Road is to be cleared and developed with more than 2,000 dwellings.

STRIKING

Through the centre of the new development will run a kind of "spine," with two rows of dwellings, one of four storeys and one of six storeys. Beneath it will be car parking and probably private open space.

To either side of the spine will be single-storey, two-storey and a few three storey homes, and the whole estate will be on the traffic-free system. Pedestrians will, as far as possible, be kept away from roads. One striking point is that skyscraper blocks are not marked on the plan — the new estate will not be developed with this kind of dwelling.

Joseph Williams School, I was told, is about the only one of the older buildings which is being left alone. In fact, it will probably benefit from the redevelopment by being given a slice of land to use as playing fields.

The new area will have a "local centre," as planners have called the proposed development for the centre of the estate. It will include a supermarket, a civic laundry, community building and other facilities.

The whole development, which will be "home" to about 6,500 people, will supplement the large "district centre" on the other side of Childwall Valley Road, where prefabs in the other separate section are still standing. The district centre will cater for everything from shopping to entertainment, and it will be the first of about ten district centres planned for the entire city.

The Belle Vale District Centre is very much a thing of the future, but the multi-million pound housing development on the now demolished prefab estate could begin quite soon.

How soon is difficult to say, but optimists say a start could be made by the end of the year. Main difficulty is bringing down the cost of the scheme to a figure which is acceptable to the Government. Until then, the old prefab sites are likely to remain a tangle of weeds and broken bricks.

Hidden away behind overgrown hedges and long grass is the home of the Pinnington family, 175 Cloverdale Road. Around this solitary prefab are the crumbling foundations of former homes.

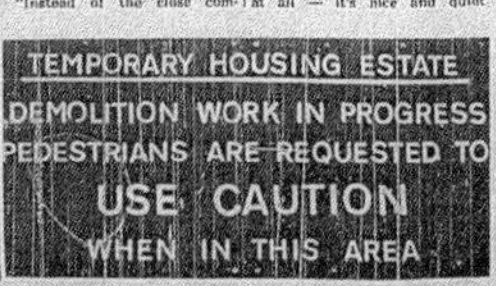

This sign was put up when demolition work began on the prefab site. The "Temporary Housing Estate" lasted twice its proposed lifetime — it should have come down in the mid-1950s.

A bird's-eye view of the demolished estate shows the Joseph Williams County Primary School in the foreground and a single prefab almost hidden from view on the right. The school is the only main building which will remain in the future development of the prefab site. In the morning haze on the sky-line are the sky-scraper flats of Childwall Valley which marked the beginning of the end for the prefab people of Belle Vale.

FINED £80 ON INDECENCY CHARGES

Ernest Carr Whittingham, aged 58, of 8a Tiverton Road, Halewood, was given a six months suspended prison sentence and fined a total of £80 at Widnes Magistrates' Court last Thursday when he admitted indecently assaulting two girls, one aged 11 and the other 12, and committing an act of gross indecency with the 12-year-old and with another girl, also aged 12.

Whittingham, a head stageman at Tranmere Oil Terminal, said in court: "I'm very sorry that it's all happened. I am disgusted with myself and glad it has come into the open."

Inspector R. Berry, prosecuting, told the magistrates that defendant had been indecent towards two girls aged 12 years and one aged 11, and had asked for six similar offences to be taken into consideration. The offences had occurred between January and June of this year, and were committed in the defendant's home, he said.

Sixty years ser[...] at the "Florr[...]

A WELL KNOWN local figure, Mr. Trevo[...] has been connected with youth work [...] life, was guest of honour at a dinner held b[...] Institute Boys' Club in the Tudor Rooms on Thursday evening.

Mr. Holden has been part of the Florence Institute for more than 60 years. He was first taken to the club as a small boy by his father and has been in the club since. He has been chief helper to the boys, chairman of the Board of Managers and president, secretary and treasurer of the Institute.

Mr. Holden is a past president of the Magistrates' Board and has been a city magistrate for many years.

At the dinner, Mr. Holden said that his work with the boys in the Institute had helped him a great deal in understanding the many people who had appeared before the Magistrates' bench.

After the dinner, Paula Cooper, a young helper at the Institute, presented Mr. Holden with an engraved silver sweet dish and gave Mrs. Holden a bouquet of flowers as a mark of appreciation of the staff of the Florence Institute.

Mr. and Mrs. Holden, who live in Grassendale, hope to move shortly to Jamaica and will be taking with them the silver sweet dish to remind them of their connections with the Institute.

To be turned into nursery

Part of Dingle House, South Hill Road, once used by the city's Libraries Committee, is to be turned into a nursery for handicapped children.

Houses on R.A.F. site

The former 25-acre R.A.F. site in Fazakerley is to be used for providing more than 540 two-storey houses and three-four storey cluster blocks.

Clean car site

A car wash, along with stores and offices, is to be built on land adjoining the garage at 308-310 Kensington.

Emerg[...] Chem[...]

Chemists op[...] gency services [...] during the w[...] Monday, Augu[...]

Monday to [...] to 7 p.m.: Ha[...] 97 Westminste[...] Cullen, 74 Pri[...] Harris (Chem[...] Smith Street; [...] Lappin Ltd., [...] Street; Melca[...] (Liverpool) Ltd[...] Avenue; W. I. [...] Moss Lane; E[...] Eaton Road; [...] 99 Green Lane[...] kin and Son[...] Parade; E. H. [...] High Street; J. [...] Childwall Abbe[...] Hull, 17 Bo[...] Boots The Ch[...] Allerton Road; [...] Garston Old [...] Pharmacy, 31 [...] M. Rosenfeld, [...] Avenue.

Saturday 6 [...] and Sunday 12 [...] I. Turnpenny ([...] 251 County Ro[...] ton, 49 Stanley[...] Cooper, 503 [...] Road; W. Bry[...] Street; C. La[...] 344 Edge Lan[...] (Liverpool) L[...] Road; Martin [...] Lodge Lane; [...] Longmoor Lane[...] (Liverpool) Lt[...] way; E. H. G[...] Road; J. H. Pa[...] Road; J. W. [...] Picton Road; H[...] ter (Chemists[...] Aigburth Road; [...] Booker Avenue[...] Lewis Ltd., 14 [...] J. S. Pendlebu[...] Street.

CHRISTIAN[...]

"Spirit" is the [...] Lesson-Sermon [...] Science churche[...]

Among Bible [...] cluded in the L[...] a verse from II[...] God hath not gi[...] of fear; but of [...] love, and of a so[...]

Belle Vale Gallery

"People from many walks of life contributed to the community"

Liverpool Education Committee

OFFICIAL OPENING
OF THE
JOSEPH WILLIAMS
COUNTY PRIMARY
SCHOOL
BELLE VALE

Monday 30th October
at 2·30 p.m.   1950

Joseph Williams School, 1957.

Second row, far left: Jean Young: Bottom row, far left: Vicky Green
Bottom row, far right: Pat Jolliffe, Susan Wooldridge.
Also on photo: Julie Cooper, Irene Nancollis, Linda Dawber, Valerie Davidson, Michelle Rooney,
Gail Tinman, Edith Burbridge, Billy Evans, Lesley Light, Joe Barker.

Hazel Prenton, age 6 (centre with bow), Joseph Williams School

Belle Vale School Summer Holiday, Ramsey, Isle of Man, 1960.
Do you recognise anybody?

READER Eddie Bolton of Liverpool 17 sent us this photograph of 10 sets of twins who all attended Joseph Williams primary school, Childwall, around 1953. Edward and his twin sister Ruth are pictured but does anyone recognise anyone else? Eddie says: "There must have been a baby boom around five years before this picture was taken, judging by all the twins!".

Twins at Joseph Williams School, 1953

Joseph Williams championship soccer team, 1960

The only school in Liverpool ever to win the Horne Brothers League Cup and the Hanson Knock Out Cup in the same season. Both matches were within three days. That season the team scored 98 goals for only 9 against.

Team members: Left to Right, front row: Teacher and Coach Mr. K. Herbert, John McCubbon, Stephen Curry, Kevin Wilson, Brian Corson, Keith Kewley. Back row, from left: Raymond Cooke, Alan Jones, Thomas Quayle, George Smith, Robert Kirkwood, Mike Otterson, Terence McNerney (reserve).

Belle Vale Youth Club

School Trip to Devil's Bridge

THE CAMP PARTY.

The Camp Address is:

Name
  Belle Vale School,
    H. F. Pencoed Youth Camp,
      Devil's Bridge,
        Aberystwyth,
          Cardiganshire.

Date: Friday 25th July
            to
       Friday 1st August.

Pocket Money.

   From experience it has been found that £1 is quite sufficient spending money It is not necessary to take £1 - this is the maximum.

   The leader in charge of your group will look after your money and you may draw it out each morning.

Mr Headey	Mrs. Headey
J. Allen	K. Forsyth
F. Armstrong	D. Griffin.
N. Bainbridge	G. Gardner
K. Bainbridge	R. Guy.
J. Buchanan.	T. Horne.
P. Buchanan.	A. Headey.
S. Buchanan.	I. Headey.
P. Crookham.	R. Jackson.

Mr. Roberts.	Mr. Davies.
T. Kelly	D. Squires.
G. McCulloch.	R. Stephenson.
W. McQuillan.	K. Thompson.
K. Meadows.	A. Wallace.
T. Meadows	J. Wallace.
G. Molloy.	P. Ward.
R. Norton.	J. Whittaker.
T. Rowlands.	

Miss Davis.	Miss Ensor.
C Byrom	J. Jackson
G. Chaloner	E. Johnson.
A. Davies.	G. Jones.
M. Evans	M. McDonald.
Linda Hiesley	C. Turner.
S. Hogan.	P. Winter.
C. Sudlow.	

Belle Vale School Camp Party at Devil's Bridge

Belle Vale School Play

Miss Alice Howard, Deputy Head Teacher of Joseph Williams School 1950 - 1973.
Taken Jan 2006

Belle Vale School class photo

Music Lesson 1952, Belle Vale School

L-R Kevin Patterson, Jackie, Linda & Sheila Woods. Rest unknown

Park Vale Football Team

Park Vale Football Team was formed in 1961, when Belle Vale Community Centre closed down.

Belle Vale Community Centre ran two football teams, Belle Vale seniors and juniors. Kenny Morris, Tony Givnan and Billy Taylor with the help of Mr Willis and Mr Cross formed a new team. Some of the lads had already moved to Lee Park and some were still in Belle Vale, so the new team were called Park Vale.

We only had one kit and one game when our colours clashed with the other team, we had to wear our best white Saturday night shirts. As shown in the photograph.
Peter Morris
7 Cloverdale Rd

Back row left to right
Peter Morris, Kenny Owen, Brian Knight, Robbie Nancollis, Tommy Curtis.

Front row left to right
Tony Givnan, Billy Taylor, Kenny Morris, Joey Farlow,
Keith Hall, Tony Hunter.

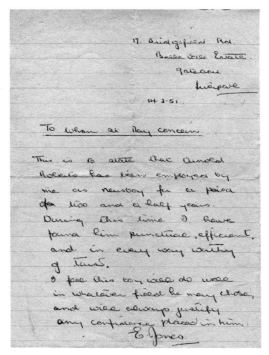

Paperboy Reference for Arnie Roberts. 93 Whinhurst Rd

Carol Maher, Helen Humphries, Pat Ryan, Elsie Griffiths, Philomena Carol, Maureen Campbell, Mary Gedeher, Ann Turner, Doris Flynn, Claire Bleasdale, Denise Higgins, Necer Hills, Jean Browne, Maria Williams, Mary Joyce.

Mr Prickett delivering milk to the prefabs.

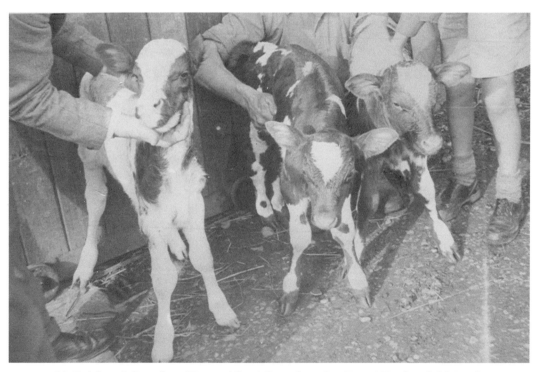

Mr Prickett & Daughter Mary with triplet calves. Ivy Farm, Naylorsfield Road.
Mr Prickett delivered milk to the prefab estate.

THIS SLIP SHOULD BE AFFIXED TO THE PRINTED "NOTES FOR THE TENANTS OF TEMPORARY HOUSES" WITH WHICH YOU HAVE ALSO BEEN SUPPLIED.

ALUMINIUM HOUSES.

The particular attention of tenants of aluminium temporary houses is drawn to the following special points.

Windows. Do not slam windows or hang articles on the handles or stays. Do not use abrasives or metal polish on unpainted aluminium windows—they should be cleaned in the same way as the glass.

Paintwork. Do not clean with abrasives—soap and water should be used. The paintwork on the outside walls acts as a protective to the aluminium and care should be taken not to damage it.

Cupboards. Care should be taken with cupboard doors to avoid damage to hinges. Do not hang articles on doors.

Wireless. A wireless aerial is provided and **tenants should not, in any circumstances, fit their own outside aerial.**

(32183)   Wt.30133/9100   60,000   10/46   A.& E.W.Ltd.   Gp.745

Aluminium Houses

Back Door Key for France Family, 31 Charlwood Rd

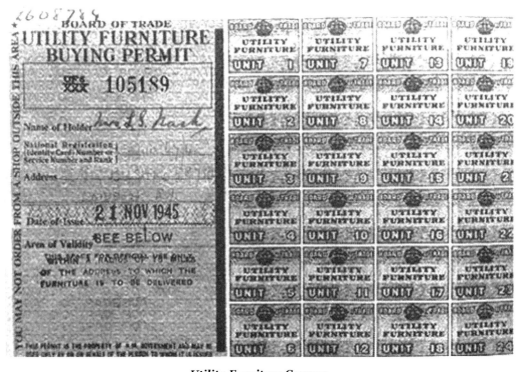

Utility Furniture Coupon

Paul Robinson, apprentice at Hedgefield Road barbers

Michael Fitzmaurice remembers 'I lived at 9 Lineside Road with my parents and brothers Patrick and Dermot Fitzmaurice. I saw the picture of Mr. McCormack the barber in "Prefab Days" and remembered his apprentice Paul Robinson who had his shop in Lark Lane. Here is a photo of Paul with the book.'

Childrens Party, Labour Club

The Labour Club

Harry Robertson's dad, an electrician, 'was one of the many tradesmen who provided labour free to build a Labour Club on the site of today's Millennium Centre' (as he tells us in "Prefab Days" page 47). Chuck and John Smith's dad was responsible for digging the footings and the cellar. The Crowleys were the bricklayers, as was Sandy Thomas. Bob Unsworth, a joiner, built the bar and the wood fittings.
Harry Robertson
2 Endbrook Road

Labour Club, 1955

Vic Symons - Resident drummer at the Labour Club

Labour Club Demolished

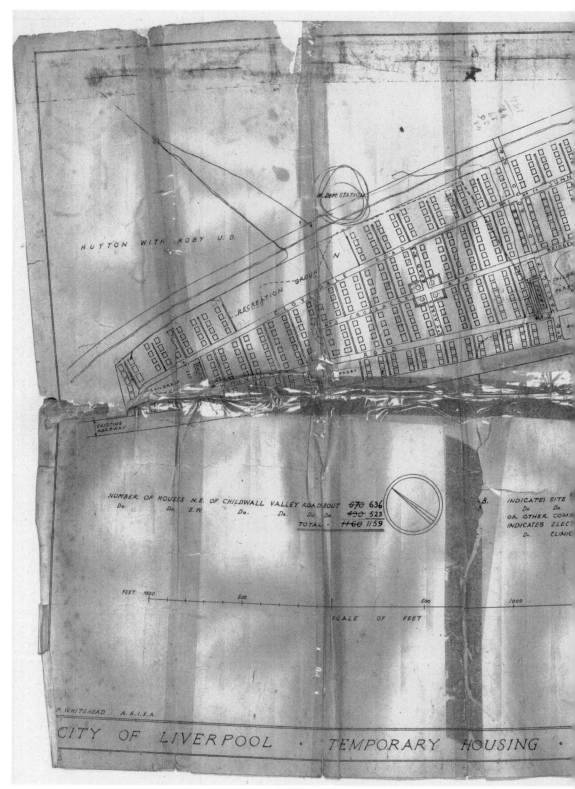

CITY OF LIVERPOOL · TEMPORARY HOUSING ·

This is the original plan of the Belle Vale e
Lancelot Keay's name is the bottom right

VALE ESTATE · GATEACRE ·

RECREATION GROUND

GARAGE

BRIDGE INN

BELLE VALE PUMPING STATION

COMMUNITY HALL

LEE PARK

RECREATION GROUND

CHARLWOOD ROAD

BELLE

ROAD

FARMING FACTORY

ST. STEPHENS CHURCH

BELLE VALE COTTAGE

CAMBO LANE

SITE RESERVED FOR SCHOOL

AMENITY BUILDING.
NURSERY SCHOOL
NG.
TION SITES.

SHOPS

BIRKSIDE

GELLAMORE ROAD

BELLE VUE ROAD

CHILDREN'S PLAYGROUND

CHESHIRE LINES RAILWAY

PUBLIC FOOTPATH

GATEACRE & WOOLTON STATION

AMENDED 29.5.46

DRAWING Nº TH/15 (REVISED)

L H KEAY · M. ARCH., F.R.I.B.A.
CITY ARCHITECT AND DIRECTOR
OF HOUSING · 4·8·1945

m the City Council Architects Department.
iven to the project by the Prenton family.

103

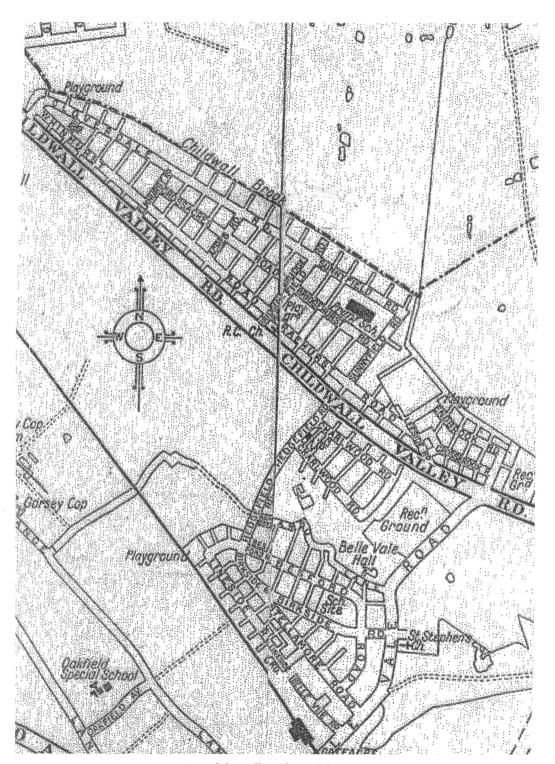

Map of the Belle Vale Prefab Estate

Some of the Belle Vale Prefab Project members who went to visit the prefab at the National Museum of Architecture, Saint Fagan's, Cardiff. 2006

The interiors as shown in the following photos are similar to the prefabs on the Belle Vale estate.

Living Room

Bathroom

Kitchen

THE PREFABS

How happy we were to live there
In our prefab days!
What a far cry it was from today
In many, many ways.
There was always the Coronation
And the T.A. Barracks too.
We had a brook ran through the field
With nothing to spoil the view.
We used to play upon the field
With family and friends
On glorious beautiful sunny days
That never seemed to end.

The community and the spirit
Was really beyond compare
And if you had a problem
Your neighbour was always there.
There were not many shops around that time
But often a van did come
With bread and things you needed
And at Easter, a Hot Cross Bun.

The children's education
Depended on five schools
And you were severely punished
If you dared to break the rules.
The prefabs were not really very big
But as a child it played a part
With many happy memories
That are forever in my heart.

I remember in the winter
They used to get so cold
And I am sure people have many tales to tell
Of times gone by, of old
When people seemed to respect each other
And doors were left ajar
Where neighbours popped in for some tea
Now a memory just so far.

We will always remember the prefabs
And the happy times we had.
To have lived there was a privilege
And it always makes me glad
To say I was a resident
And will always be proud to be
Of that generation
And of that community.

By Sandra Nairen, 70 Cloverdale Road

INVESTORS

Ken Lawrence

Pat Douglas

Jean Young

Vicky Green

Nellie Rigby

Diane Allen

Dorothy James

Janet Walsh

David Mowat

John Smith

Micheal Fitzmaurice

Tony Hunter

Sandra Sandland

Ernie Benstead

Frank Lawrence

Eric Smith

Irene Spiers

Edna Corness

Sandra Nairen

Sue Glover

Anne Collins

Don Headey

Peter Morris

Reg Owen

James Thompson

Magaret Cannon

Tom Foster

Pamela Foster

Muriel Ellis

Alan Prescot

Phil Young

Barbara Hall

Ruth Roberts

Dorcas Rowles

Carol Barr

Jean Downey

Sue Wilding

Chuck Smith

G. Moore

Peter Heys

Doreen Bruffell

Celia Kelly

Sandra Harrison

Eddie Lansdowne

Arnie Roberts

Ray Percival

Linda Thomas

Harold Robertson

June Dawber

Norman Downs

Harry Potter

Barbara Myers

Freda Heathcote

Maureen Davies

Paul Carey

Sue Carey

James Pettitt

Charlie France

Rob France

Raymond Kayll